The Instant Manager

Revised Edition

The Instant Manager

More Than 100 Quick Tips and Techniques for Great Results

Revised Edition

Cy Charney

American Management Association

New York • Atlanta • Brussels • Chicago • Mexico City • San Francisco
Shanghai • Tokyo • Toronto • Washington, D.C.

Special discounts on bulk quantities of AMACOM books are
available to corporations, professional associations, and other
organizations. For details, contact Special Sales Department,
AMACOM, a division of American Management Association,
1601 Broadway, New York, NY 10019.
Tel.: 212-903-8316. Fax: 212-903-8083.
Web site: www.amacombooks.org

This publication is designed to provide accurate and authoritative
information in regard to the subject matter covered. It is sold with
the understanding that the publisher is not engaged in rendering
legal, accounting, or other professional service. If legal advice or
other expert assistance is required, the services of a competent
professional person should be sought.

Library of Congress Cataloging-in-Publication Data
Charney, Cyril.
     The instant manager : more than 100 quick tips and techniques for great results / Cy
Charney. — Rev. ed.
        p. cm.
     Previous ed. in LC under title : The manager's tool kit.
     Includes bibliographical references and index.
     ISBN 0-8144-7213-3
     1. Management—Handbooks, manuals, etc.   2. Leadership—Handbooks, manuals, etc.
I. Title.
     HD38.15.C474 2004
     658.4'03—dc22   2004003416

Previous editions of this book were published by Stoddart Publishing Co., Limited, Toronto,
Canada, and under the title The Manager's Tool Kit by AMACOM,
a division of American Management Association.

The performance indexing system used in "Measuring Team Performance"
is based on the objective matrix system described in Productivity by
Objectives by James L. Riggs and Glenn H. Felix, Englewood Cliffs, NJ: Prentice Hall,
1983.

Printing number
10 9 8 7 6 5 4 3 2

To Yael Adi Haas, My Grandchild

Your entry into the world was dramatic and traumatic,
But you were determined to overcome all obstacles,
As if you knew how much we cared and prayed for you.

And now that you're one year old,
Know how much joy you bring into our world.

When your eyes search for me when I'm near,
Or you smile so broadly when I call,
Or touch my cheek so gently,
Or pull my hair, squealing with delight,
Know that nothing brings me as much joy as you.
Nothing!

Contents

Preface

*T*his book is designed to enable you to quickly access tools you need to be an effective manager. If you have attended many training sessions but need to brush up on selected skills, it will be a reminder to you of skills you may have forgotten. Or you may need a mentor to provide you with information and tools to improve your performance quickly.

In developing this book I have relied on the tools I have taught managers in Canada, the United States, Europe and Africa. My approach has been pragmatic, offering managers tools and techniques that I have used or have seen work in client organizations.

Throughout the book I approach the issue of management from the philosophy that 99% of employees are responsible, are enthusiastic about contributing to the goals of the organization, are loyal, and want to expand their influence. This has certainly been my experience. The challenge for managers, then, is to find out what roadblocks stand in the way of superior performance and to remove those roadblocks.

This book has many of the solutions.

Much has changed since the printing of the first edition of *The Instant Manager* in 1994 and its U.S. edition (entitled *The Manager's Tool Kit*) in 1995. These new business realities have prompted me to update the material, adding new tools that work in a virtual world. Most organizations are feeling the pressures of time — hence they rely more on the electronic transfer of information through e-mails, the Internet and virtual meetings. The need to bring people up to speed without sending them out on courses requires an increasing amount of coaching and mentoring on the job. And more organizations are focusing on their core strengths and forming partnerships with others who can provide non-core services —hence the proliferation of outsourcing.

Sadly, many managers say they believe in their people, but their leadership styles reflect distrust. To improve performance, people in positions of leadership need to spend more time coaching and mentoring their people—training them, measuring their performance, constantly providing feedback, celebrating success, problem solving their challenges. These and many other tools are the stuff of which this book is made. *The Instant Manager* will help you unlock human potential.

PART I

Personal Growth

Career Management

My grandfather once told me that there are two kinds of people: those who do the work and those who take the credit. He told me to try and be in the first group: there was less competition there.

INDIRA GANDHI (1917–84)

Careers need to be managed as much as people do. Your career can benefit from the same skills you bring to project management, team leadership and conflict resolution. And, as in all of the former, your approach must be pro-active — wait for your career to manage itself and you'll likely wait forever. Use the following tips to make career opportunities for yourself:

- Be a team player and make your best effort to shine on the team. Encourage others to reach team goals on time and within budget.
- Volunteer for high-profile projects. Doing so will increase your exposure to key decision makers.
- Stay out of political camps. If you have to make a choice, wait as long as you can to increase your chances of backing the winner.
- Conduct yourself with integrity both on and off the job. Tell the truth no matter how difficult it may be. As Mark Twain said, "this will gratify some people and astonish the rest." Everyone wants to work for, and with, people they can trust.
- Always work collaboratively. Running others down or refusing to co-operate will only lead to senseless conflict. Your chances of a promotion are slim when you are continuously in the centre of controversy.

- Think like a top manager. Stay in tune with the "hot buttons" of the day and find ways to help meet corporate objectives. If there are critical roadblocks preventing the organization from moving forward, look for ways in which these can be removed.
- Establish a joint vision with your boss of your career objectives and the road by which you will obtain them.
- Let your boss know your career goals. Ask whether your goals are realistic, whether you have the skills to achieve your goals, and what training you should take to improve yourself.
- Develop action plans that are goal-oriented. Review the goals and mini-goals regularly to see if you are on track. If you are not, evaluate your steps and adjust your plan accordingly.
- Find a mentor. Identify someone in the organization who is well regarded and whom you admire, someone who complements your skills and traits. When you are faced with difficult situations seek advice, or ask your mentor to evaluate your decisions.
- Project a "can do" approach. Don't burden others with problems, doubts and roadblocks. Speak about opportunities and solutions, not problems.
- Always be positive; think of the glass as half full rather than half empty. Remember: more people are fired for poor attitudes than for any other reason.
- Focus your energy on jobs that will
  - ✓ best use your skills
  - ✓ have the greatest chance of success
  - ✓ require an optimal amount of effort and resources
- Do, and be seen to be doing, things that help your organization:
  - ✓ Pass on sales leads.
  - ✓ Look for and suggest ways to reduce costs.
  - ✓ Become a source of information. Keep up with news trends by scanning business and trade publications. Circulate materials to people who can benefit.
  - ✓ Undertake less popular assignments.

- If unpleasant news is on the way, let your boss know first and early. Nobody wants unpleasant surprises, particularly ones that might embarrass them.
- Know what your boss expects of you. If possible, agree on measurable goals so that your achievements are indisputable.
- Ask for more authority and autonomy. Stretch yourself. Take on more than you think you are capable of to prove to yourself, and others, what you can do.
- Compete against yourself and let others judge whether you are better than your peers. Competing against your peers will increase their resentment towards you. You will become the subject of sniping and back-stabbing.
- Be willing to accept criticism. The critique will be most effective if you do the following:
  - ✓ Control your emotions. Don't be defensive. Be objective.
  - ✓ Put yourself in the critic's place. Would you take a similar view?
  - ✓ Treat each criticism as an opportunity to learn and grow.
  - ✓ Defend yourself if, after reflection, you feel that your evaluation was unfair.
  - ✓ Thank the person giving the criticism, even if you disagree with the content.
- Learn from setbacks. You will get no benefit from blaming others or continuing to be angry. Find out what you did wrong. Try, as hard as it may be, to be objective. Above all, fix the problem and focus your energies on avoiding the same mistake.
- Acknowledge the help of others publicly. This will increase your network of supporters.
- Learn to get what you want, while still being liked. Don't alienate important people since you never know when they could be influential in picking the next person to be promoted.
- Sign up for workshops, seminars, discussion groups, or whatever else you see as skill-enhancing.

- If you sense that a desirable job will be available in the foreseeable future, make yourself a leading contender by
  - ✓ taking on extra work to demonstrate your skill in that job
  - ✓ letting the right people know of your interest
  - ✓ updating the skills and knowledge required for the job
- Never stop learning. In our information age, we should all consider ourselves lifelong students. Sign up for any related training or courses that your organization provides, both onsite and off. And let it be known at work that you're the consummate perennial student.

Career Planning

Every exit is an entry somewhere else.

TOM STOPPARD, ENGLISH PLAYWRIGHT

*W*hen it comes to planning your career, the operative word is YOU. No one knows better than you where your talents and your dreams lie, and how and where you see yourself down the road. A little long-term planning goes a long way. In today's business climate of relentless restructuring and downsizing, it's imperative that we each assume responsibility for our own job futures. Gone are the days when we can expect Big Brother to take our hands and show us the way.

- In setting your goals, by all means dream big! But do frequent reality checks as well.
- Zero in on specific career goals, and define the exact steps for reaching each of them, complete with timetables and to-do lists. Visualize your path, and determine how you'll reach each milestone.
- To enhance your personal and professional worth, become a "forward thinker," and gain recognition as one. Don't get stuck in ruts, or fall back on hackneyed clichés and worn-out ideas. Think beyond!
- Get out there. Join your fellow professionals at conferences and within associations.
- Read anything and everything you can about your current professional domain.
- Harness the power of the Net. Find out where your peers are on the Web and join them in chat rooms and at associations' web

sites. The Net is simply an unbeatable resource for job-specific information and contacts, and leading-edge developments in your particular field. Today, you cannot afford to ignore it.

- Be an agent of change, and be known as such. Pioneer the introduction of new ideas and technologies.
- Find ways to keep your interest, energy and enthusiasm high. Focus on the leading edge in your actions and discussions, both on and off the job.
- Continuously update your resumé so that it incorporates all your best achievements.
- Make your resumé sing!
  - ✓ First, away with all modesty! Include details of your finest achievements, specifically projects that contributed to the all-important bottom line.
  - ✓ Spend some time and money, if necessary, on its design. No one will know how great you are unless they read your resumé! With the tools now available on computers, we can all become graphic designers. Consider using colour, highlighting, shadow boxes and more. Let your creativity shine through.
  - ✓ Double-check grammar, spelling and details.
  - ✓ Above all else, be truthful.
- Create your own web site. Include your electronic resumé. Highlight your achievements in any number of electronic formats, including photos, graphics, animation, even interactive content! If the task seems daunting, and admittedly it can be for the uninitiated, there are innumerable tools online to walk you through it. Or consider contacting community colleges, which turn out web site designers with the latest know-how on all the bells and whistles cyberspace has to offer.
- Determine exactly what you are worth in the marketplace. That way, you'll know whether you're adequately paid in your current job, and what you can justify asking for in your next one. How do you define your value? Answer these three questions:

✓ How great is the need for what I do?

✓ Am I easily replaced?

✓ How good am I at what I do?

- Divide a sheet of paper into two columns. Title one column "Strengths," the other, "Weaknesses." (It is hoped that the former will be slightly longer than the latter!) For help here, ask the people whom you trust and who know you best.

- Define what it is that makes you indispensable to your organization. If you can't honestly come up with something, make that a distinct goal now. Isolate that one thing that you alone can offer an organization, and offer it with all the gusto you have. For example, is your company expanding to the Far East? Study the markets, language and customs there and talk them up with your colleagues.

- Get to know professionals outside your field of expertise. The Net is an invaluable tool here. Include a variety of recruiters, consultants, pioneers and entrepreneurs among your ongoing contacts. Open yourself up to a wider world. Job leads and ideas come from the most unlikely sources.

- Most often neglected in any career planning primer are the genuinely underrated and overlooked powers of humour, humility, congeniality and kindness in your professional conduct. You'll be amazed at the results they bring!

Changing Careers

*You have to take control over your own life, or
someone else will do it for you.*

ANONYMOUS

C orporations have globalized, rationalized, downsized and out-
sourced their way into the twenty-first century, with the result
that the team you supervise, department you run or project you
manage can change character overnight or even pass out of existence
altogether.

Along with the rapid rate of change comes a change in career
strategy. Nowadays it is possible — and even likely — that the
perfect job you were hired for has become an entirely different,
burdensome task after a given merger/rationalization/purge. Don't
be surprised, we tell recent college grads, if you have as many as six
careers during your lifetime.

This now applies to everyone, including you.

Are you aching for a change? Answer these questions:
- **Who am I?** You at 20, 30, 40 and 50 would be four people who
  could not necessarily even have a civil conversation in a bar. It is
  not surprising that the job that suited you fine as little as two
  years ago can chafe now; often what has changed is you.
- **What do I value?** Honesty, loyalty, friendliness, integrity and
  justice are popular choices, but the question also refers to political and religious beliefs and cultural and societal norms. When
  your employees and higher-ups violate these beliefs, or the
  organization itself requires that you violate them, you will find it
  difficult to work productively. If your value requirements are not

being met at your present job, it is probably time to leave.

- **What skills do I have?** This goes beyond the keyboarding speed and office applications that got your foot in the door:
  - ✓ Are you good at supervising people?
  - ✓ Do you learn quickly?
  - ✓ Have you always had a flair for design, or copy writing, or computer programming?

  Keep an up-to-date inventory of special and commonplace skills — it's not just for college grads anymore — and add to them whenever possible. Can you use Quark or PhotoShop, even though you manage a meat packing plant? Then you could be an editor of a trade magazine. Listing your skills will help you think laterally of careers that may never have even occurred to you, and will hint at what skill sets you should pick up to make just the right company come headhunting for you.

- **How daring am I?** Did you jump off the high diving board as a kid? Would you now? Our risk-aversion level changes as we mature, and the you who thought nothing of eating only macaroni and cheese while searching for that big break may shudder now at having to dig into the savings to finance a job search.

- **What do I really want to do?** Along with changes in personal outlook and values go changes in career aspirations. Perhaps you would prefer a position with a bit more stability and less running around than seemed attractive when you were starting out. Perhaps you want to be more active, more engaged. The point is, you have probably shifted your priorities, and you need to rediscover them.

- **How active do you want to be?** Do you like to travel? Do you like sitting behind a desk? What kind of work would you like to be on that desk? If you can't be sure how to answer these questions in under, say, 10 seconds, it's time to take a good hard look at what you really want to be doing with your work time.

- **How patient am I?** Do you have the endurance to engage in a protracted job hunt to find just the right position for you? You may have been in your current position for enough time to forget the frustration of looking for a job. Talk to a headhunter in your chosen field about what the job market is like, how far afield you may have to go and how long a job search is likely to take. Then decide whether your finances and your psyche can handle it. You may wish to sit tight instead and wait for a better market situation before taking the plunge.

- **Where am I going?** You have just re-evaluated yourself in terms of your job, now re-evaluate your job in terms of you. Can you name five positive things about the people you supervise, the work you do, the benefits your organization offers you (try not to sound like a promotion package — this is good policy most of the time, but will inhibit an honest assessment of your current job state)? Can you name five negative things? Which took less time?

Don't assume that a general feeling of malaise can be improved by jumping corporate ship — there may be other factors in your life to consider before you conclude that your career is at fault. But if you've established that you're dissatisfied with your career, you must figure out what part(s) of it you need to change:

- ✓ Are you in the right field, but at the wrong firm?
- ✓ Are you in the wrong field, but happy with your organization?
- ✓ Are you generally dissatisfied with both your area of work and your organization?
- ✓ Or do you like your field and your firm, but have problems with the people with whom you work, subordinates or superiors?

Establish whether you want a lateral internal move (within your current organization but into a different section), a lateral external move (different field, different company), a direct external (same field, different firm) or a direct internal (same job, same company, possibly shuffling around the people with whom you interact).

How do you get there? There is an obvious difference between lateral and direct career jumping, but both require research, research (and research). Use this checklist to get started:

1. Have you talked to
   ✓ people in the division of your company that you wish to enter?
   ✓ people in that division at competing companies?
   ✓ colleagues at trade shows?
   ✓ headhunters?
   ✓ a career counsellor?
   ✓ your life partner?
2. Have you read
   ✓ the job descriptions for people in your wished-for division or company?
   ✓ equivalent job descriptions in other firms?
   ✓ trade publications on the latest advances in techniques and technology in your new chosen field?
   ✓ annual reports and background information on your organi-zation(s) of choice?
3. Have you updated
   ✓ your skill set?
   ✓ your resumé?
   ✓ your skill set as listed on your resumé?
   ✓ your data base with all the contacts you just made?

Career jumping can take you back to when you were first starting out, but it doesn't have to. Keep in mind that you have been in a position of responsibility for some years now, despite being currently dissatisfied with it, and that you have learned an essential skill — how to manage people. Between your managerial skills, your training in your current field and following the checklist above, you will find that even a lateral move can be surprisingly easy.

THINGS TO AVOID IN A JOB INTERVIEW

Your chances of a job offer will be significantly reduced if you
- ✓ are not dressed and groomed properly
- ✓ show little interest in or enthusiasm for the job
- ✓ criticize your previous employer
- ✓ emphasize the importance of money
- ✓ fail to maintain eye contact
- ✓ project yourself as indecisive, nervous and ill at ease
- ✓ fail to project an interest in a career
- ✓ cannot express yourself clearly
- ✓ don't speak with a firm, clear voice
- ✓ project conceit, over-aggressiveness or superiority
- ✓ fail to ask about the job
- ✓ are late for the interview
- ✓ expect too high a position or salary relative to your background and skills
- ✓ indicate you are shopping around
- ✓ fail to complete the application form properly
- ✓ don't live up to expectations suggested by your resumé
- ✓ don't provide direct answers to questions

What to Do if You Get Fired

If you aren't fired with enthusiasm, you will be fired with enthusiasm.

VINCE LOMBARDI (1913–70), FOOTBALL COACH

*A*s many companies continue to flatten their structures to become more effective and reduce costs, laying off managers is commonplace. If you are caught in the restructuring, make the best of a bad situation by doing the following:

At the Exit Interview

- Do not show anger or resort to blaming anyone. A collaborative but firm attitude will allow you to depart gracefully, with as much dignity and cash as possible.
- Don't sign any release or settlement documentation until it is fair and reasonable. If you are unsure, consult a labour lawyer. The guideline of one week's pay for every year of service is a start, but you may be able to negotiate more (see Negotiating — Power Strategies, page 30).
- Seek outplacement services as part of your severance package. A counselling service can provide you with
  - ✓ personality and skills assessment
  - ✓ resumé skills
  - ✓ interview coaching
  - ✓ contacts ·
  - ✓ guidance on a broad range of job strategies
- A counsellor can help you come to terms with your situation, act as a sounding board for new ideas, and help you turn adversity into opportunity. If you are able to work out of an outplacement

service's office, you will be able to keep up a daily routine and make your transition less stressful.

Later

- Come to terms with your situation by sharing your pain with those closest to you. Releasing your anger and frustration verbally will enable you to refocus on the rest of your life.
- Develop a network of contacts. Go through your diaries and business cards and make a list of people to contact. You never know who can offer you a job, an idea or a lead.
- Write a resumé that, while being accurate, will excite people with the possibility of employing you. Your resumé should be short, accurate and pertinent. It should also
  - ✓ focus on a specific job
  - ✓ highlight your strengths
  - ✓ appeal aesthetically
- Meet with people who have worked with you professionally. Seek their feedback on your strengths and weaknesses. Plan to deal with your shortcomings so that you will be even more valuable to your next employer than you were to the last.
- Fantasize about what you would love to do, irrespective of practical realities such as money or location. Find out about those jobs from people in the field, asking specifically how they got those jobs. Evaluate whether you have the time, patience and confidence to make a career change.
- Set up a plan to get as many job offers as possible. Put aside time each day for
  - ✓ reviewing and responding to newspaper advertisements
  - ✓ calling people in your network
  - ✓ sending out targeted broadcast letters
- Sharpen your interview skills. It would be a tragedy if you got an interview and then blew the opportunity to get a job offer (see "Things to Avoid in a Job Interview," page 14). Practise with a counsellor or a confidant.

Assertiveness

To know how to refuse is as important as to know how to consent.

BALTASAR GRACIÁN (1601–58),
SPANISH WRITER AND JESUIT PRIEST

*A*ssertiveness is confidence translated into action. It is neither bullying nor brow-beating, but is simply allowing your convictions to carry a conversation. Honesty combined with a nonconfrontational manner will make assertiveness one of the most valuable tools in your managerial kit.

- Project confident body language. Actors know that physical actions and expressions of an emotion lead them to an actual experience of the emotion.
  - ✓ Lean towards the person you are influencing.
  - ✓ Get into his space.
  - ✓ Don't slouch.
  - ✓ Make and maintain eye contact (if this makes you nervous at first, stare at the bridge of the person's nose until you feel comfortable meeting her gaze).
  - ✓ If you sit, place your hands on the table and don't fidget. If you stand, don't pace. Stillness projects confidence.
- Speak with authority. Assertive people enunciate, allowing each carefully articulated point to make an impact on their audience before they move on. Speak clearly, and always address someone in particular rather than the air.
- Take ownership of issues. Make them yours by using "I" statements. Couple this with letting people know how you feel about

the issues. ("I feel upset.") Stick to the point, and end on a strong note; don't dwindle off, saying "and so on" or "et cetera."

- Confirm understandings. Build commitment to action by constantly confirming agreements to your point of view. ("Can you see why I'm upset?" or "Do you agree that this is an issue of concern?")

- Present your ideas with confidence. When you present a project schedule to your team, you have presumably put a lot of thought and planning into it. Let this show, and don't be afraid to defend the processes you've set out. Don't feel guilty about saying no. However, if someone offers a real improvement to your plan, incorporate it. That person is not "showing you up"; he is helping your overall plan succeed. Being assertive does not mean being stubborn.

- Focus. Don't get sidetracked. If you feel that the conversation is going around in circles, say so and re-state your concern — you may sound like a broken record, but you will get the discussion back on track.

- Confine the discussion to specific facts and have supporting documentation at hand.

- Don't generalize about issues. Assertiveness involves solving individual problems to your satisfaction, not making generalized accusations about a subordinate's incompetence. If a letter has a typo, say so. Do not say that someone "can't spell." Be confident that the problem can be solved, and you will inspire the confidence to get it solved.

- Maintain your authority. Never begin with an apology or an accusation. A position of authority carries certain rights and responsibilities, and the key to being assertive is finding the proper balance between them — you are neither the Tooth Fairy nor the Grim Reaper. Do not use your position of authority to silence another person prematurely, but don't keep a discussion going long after it is clear that no resolution will be reached. If you must agree to disagree, do so.

ASSERTIVENESS QUIZ

ARE YOU ASSERTIVE ENOUGH?

Do you . . .	Yes	No
1. apologize when you don't have an instant solution to a problem?	❏	❏
2. frequently apologize for your decisions?	❏	❏
3. feel that you don't have the right to change your mind?	❏	❏
4. feel guilty when you make mistakes, even when they can be fixed?	❏	❏
5. automatically say yes when someone makes a request?	❏	❏
6. feel foolish asking questions when you don't understand something?	❏	❏
7. follow instructions without question?	❏	❏
8. think your opinion doesn't count, especially if it differs from the majority?	❏	❏
9. feel that you don't have the right to ask people to change their behaviour towards you?	❏	❏
10. feel guilty delegating or deferring tasks?	❏	❏
11. have trouble walking away from an argument?	❏	❏

If you answered Yes to:

8 to 11 of the questions: You need serious improvement. Take an acting or public speaking course, review your accomplishments — whatever will boost your confidence.

4 to 7 of the questions: You're just squeaking by. Try some of the speaking and body-language techniques, and learn to keep your cool.

0 to 3 of the questions: You're just about right. Keep it up!

Influencing People

*A spoonful of honey will catch more flies than
a gallon of vinegar.*

BENJAMIN FRANKLIN (1706–90)

No matter what their rank, those in your workplace are dependent on everyone else. Every day we influence our peers, bosses and subordinates at work, and they influence us. The trick is to influence them positively, to get buy-in to your ideas and projects:

- Develop a co-operative and team-oriented outlook.
- Don't pull rank.
- Treat people with respect.
- Find out what motivates people on your team, and use it to enhance team performance.
- Deal with differences with your peers and subordinates directly — don't appeal to those above you to exert their influence, as that will keep you from developing your own.
- Understand workplace barter. Workplaces run on a formal or informal exchange of unique skills. You have some, your boss has some, your subordinates have some, and they are all different.
- Deploy your unique resources to do favours for others, ensuring that you can call on others' unique skills in return. Be sure to find out what each person's forte is, and how you can do him or her a favour to make sure you have access to that talent in the future.
- Learn to use your powers of persuasion to improve your chances of getting other people to say "Yes." Maximize your power by using a combination of

✓ **legitimacy**. Only present information for which you have considerable evidence from credible sources. Presenting the information in the form of a report will add to its weight.

✓ **precedent**. If your idea has worked in the past under similar circumstances, mention it. Point to successful pilot projects.

✓ **facts**. Gather buy-in individually from as many people as possible before generalizing an idea, and collect evidence to demonstrate their support.

✓ **expertise**. Demonstrate that you are an expert in your field — your knowledge will add to your influence. Or bring in a recognized expert, adding to the legitimacy of the idea.

✓ **rank**. Get your bosses' input on your idea. If they feel they have ownership of it, their positive opinions will carry heavy influence.

✓ **passion**. Your enthusiasm will impress those around you to take a second look at your idea.

✓ **persistence**. Don't give up on a great idea. Your tenacity will ultimately wear down opposition.

Influencing Senior Management

Strong beliefs win strong men, and then make them stronger.

WALTER BAGEHOT (1826–77),
ENGLISH ECONOMIST AND JOURNALIST

Whenever you have a great idea, you will have to sell it upwards as well as downwards. This means not only getting buy-in from your team, but from your bosses — senior management. By following a few key principles you can make the higher-ups as keen on your ideas as you are:

Prepare, prepare, prepare.

* Accumulate as much backup information as you can find. The more novel or controversial your idea, the more supporting documentation you will need.
* Rehearse your presentation beforehand with a colleague, a friend in the same field or your mentor. Remember to put together a written package to support your presentation, and have your "test audience" review it.
* Listen closely to higher-ups before pitching your idea, and incorporate some of their pet topics. If the focus of senior management is on cost-cutting, emphasize how your idea will save money. If incorporating new technology and innovations is the hot topic in your company, play on those aspects of your idea. This will increase the chances of buy-in.
* Make sure your promises and predictions or claims are realistic. Senior management can often smell snake-oil from a mile off.

Present like a pro.

- Greet the senior manager(s) warmly. Hold the hand you shake a second longer than usual (and shake firmly), and smile with your whole face.
- Project optimism. Ideas delivered cheerfully get more buy-in than those delivered in a gloomy Chicken-Littleish manner.
- Be brief and to the point. Senior managers operate under severe time constraints, and their attention spans can be quite limited. If you have a lot of supporting documentation, make up a hand-out to go with your presentation (see Written Communication, page 58).
- Listen to and show interest in their reactions, and respond to them. This will show the importance you place on their opinions.
- Give compliments when they are appropriate and where they are due. Genuine compliments, especially those on topic with your idea, will warm your audience to you and encourage further interaction.
- If you don't get immediate buy-in, determine the objections and request a follow-up meeting at which you can address them. Don't whine.

Follow up quickly.

- As soon as possible, thank those who attended your presentation in a memo. This memo should address the main issues raised at the presentation and indicate your determination to deal with them immediately.
- Gather information about outstanding objections, if there are any, and implementation, if you got immediate approval, and convey this in a report to senior management. Don't let the idea rest until a decision is made.

Conflict Between You and Others

If your neighbour does you some harm, do not pretend you are still friends . . . do not hate him, but reprove him for what he did. Through this peace can be re-established.

RASHBAM (1083–1174),
BIBLICAL SCHOLAR

Conflict is stressful. It invades and tangles your working relationships and makes every task harder. Here are ways you can address conflict:

When Conflict Occurs

- Deal with the problem right away. Don't let it fester and grow.
- Set up a time and place to sit down and resolve your differences together. Be flexible in this, accommodating the needs of others.
- Keep your meeting private.

At Your Meeting

- Create a climate for a good exchange of viewpoints. Be positive in your words and body language. Let it be known that you are determined to resolve the conflict for the sake of everyone involved.
- Make it clear that you know there are two sides to every story, and that you may be a part of the problem too.
- State your case. Be clear and firm, but not accusing. Focus on the issue, not the person. For example, "I'm upset because the report was late" is better than "You didn't give me the report on time."
- Be specific. Explain what is bothering you, but don't exaggerate.

For example, say, "I'm disappointed that the project was completed eight days late," rather than "You never get projects done on time" or "Your projects are always late."

- Watch your temper. Inflammatory language only puts the focus on your anger, not on resolving the problem.
- "Own" the problem. Use "I" statements instead of "you" statements whenever possible. For example, "I feel angry" is less likely to make a person feel defensive than "You make me angry."
- Don't harp on old problems. Stick to the current agenda.
- Listen fully to the other person's story. Don't interrupt. While you may disagree, look for points that you can agree on. Nod or gesture to show your agreement.
- Reflect back a summary of the other person's points to check your understanding. Show empathy. A statement such as "I would feel that way, too" can go a long way towards easing an angry mood, and allows you both to get on with solving the problem.
- Once the problem is understood by both sides and agreed to, move on to solutions. Offer ideas about how you could address the other person's concerns. Ask for help in addressing your own concerns. Involving the other person in solutions only increases the commitment towards resolution on both sides.
- If a resolution cannot be reached, agree to disagree. Show your respect for the view of others, even if you don't agree with it.
- Conclude your meeting with
  ✓ a brief summary of your discussion and the resulting solutions
  ✓ a statement of your appreciation for the other person's efforts to resolve your differences

After the Meeting

Keep in mind the issues raised at your meeting. Stick to your commitments. Show your appreciation when others do the same.

Appreciating Diversity

*The most practical advice for leaders is not
totreat pawns like pawns, nor princes like
princes, but all persons like persons.*

JAMES MACGREGOR BURNS,
PULITZER PRIZE–WINNING AUTHOR OF *LEADERSHIP*

*A*n increasing percentage of our workers come from countries
whose cultures are different from ours. The more we learn
about, understand and become sensitive to the differences, the better we are able to motivate people. People are motivated by unique
and respectful treatment. Here are some guidelines for managing
diversity:

- Use inoffensive terminology when referring to race or ethno-
  cultural background.
- If possible, establish a buddy system for people with similar backgrounds, at least until they establish themselves in the social
  fabric of the organization.
- In order to understand people better, learn about their ethno-
  cultural backgrounds. This information will help you understand
  their
  - ✓ greetings
  - ✓ comfort with physical closeness
  - ✓ tolerance for particular gestures
  - ✓ general attitudes towards authority and the opposite sex
  - ✓ perceptions of time and punctuality
  - ✓ attitudes towards other nationalities
  - ✓ sense of humour

- ✓ emotions
- ✓ perceptions of status (for example, the value placed on particular possessions or achievements)
- If you find that a person's sense of urgency is different from yours, point out the difference and be prepared to negotiate a solution that will be mutually acceptable.
- Be mindful of different people's comfort with physical closeness. A particular distance may be perceived as a violation of personal space by one person and as acceptable by another. Be careful when touching. A light tap on the shoulder may be acceptable in one culture and offensive in another.
- Discover each person's unique communication system. Some people find directness rude. Others find complaining or indicating a lack of understanding humiliating.
- Never allow racial slurs to go unchecked in your work area. If you do nothing, you are condoning the behaviour. People should understand that stereotypical comments are offensive and unacceptable.
- Encourage social events at which your people can get to know one another.
- Use humour to create an atmosphere of harmony among workers. Laughing at yourself will show that you are only human, giving your associates confidence when confronting you. However, racial jabs are a no-no.
- Understand that humour is used differently in different cultures. A wry sense of humour might be seen as fun in one culture but a personal affront in another.
- Find out how long people have been in your country. This information may indicate their knowledge of local customs.
- Recruit, promote, select and train people from minority groups so that they are represented in all parts and levels of your organization. Give them responsibility and authority.
- Spend more time with people of different backgrounds in order to get to know them better.

- Become aware of your body language when dealing with minorities to avoid mistaken perceptions of prejudice.
- Expect problems between visible minorities, and prepare to deal with them. Never sweep racial problems under the carpet.
- Look for opportunities to adjust work to meet your people's needs rather than always waiting for people to adjust to the job.

GENDER DIFFERENCES

Treating everyone equally and fairly is important. At the same time you need to anticipate how people feel and behave. While generalizations can be dangerous, they can act as a guide to allowing for differences. These are some typical differences.

	MEN	WOMEN
Focus	Handle single task best	Can handle more tasks simultaneously
Decisions	More comfortable with minority decisions	Prefer consensus decisions
Delegation	Prefer to tell	Prefer to ask
Use of Power	Will pull rank	Will use power of persuasion
Learning	Need theory, then practice	Prefer practice, then theory
Risk Taking	Can wing it	Want to be sure
Protection of Interest	Self	Team
Dealing with Frustration	More readily show anger	Tend to internalize anger
Patience	More likely to show impatience	Less likely to show impatience

MONOCHRONIC VS. POLYCHRONIC CULTURES

The values and customs of people who come from North American and northern and western European countries (monochronic) are different from those who come from other European, South American, African, Asian and Middle Eastern countries (polychronic). If you understand and accept the differences, you can work effectively with both groups, whatever your own background. Remember: these divisions are generalizations — there are variations within each category.

	MONOCHRONIC	POLYCHRONIC
Focus	One thing at a time Single-task dedication	Variety of things at once Easily distracted
Time	Concerned with precision e.g., 5:30 p.m.	Interest in general time e.g., after work
Punctuality	Sacred	Not sacred
Career	Me first	Us first
Planning	Follow steps religiously	Flexible
Privacy	Want individual space	Happy to share and be close to others
Sharing	Want to own tools Do not want to lend or borrow	Will share tools Happy to lend or borrow
Relationships	Short-term focus	Enduring focus
Pace	Hectic	Relaxed
Attitudes	Rigid	Flexible
Orientation	Task completion	People satisfaction

Negotiating – Power Strategies

The measure of a man is what he does with power.

PITTACUS OF MYTILENE (650–570 B.C.)

Negotiating is the ability to influence people. It is the art of letting someone else have your way. Most people have no idea how easy it is to influence others. People have a lot more power to influence than they believe they do. There are many ways you can use power to help you achieve your objective. Study and use these approaches to maximize your influence:

- **Precedent.** Show examples of where your idea has worked before. The best precedents come from your work area or organization. If you can't find examples close to home, look within your industry. When presenting ideas using precedent, say, "I know it will work because it has done so before. Here's an example . . ."
- **Legitimacy.** Make your idea look legitimate by using documentation. Written reports will enhance a verbal presentation. Information from trade journals, citing examples of success or quoting acknowledged experts will all improve your case. When you introduce legitimacy you might say, "Here is an example of what I am talking about" or "Here is additional evidence of what I am saying."
- **Persistence.** If water drops on a rock, it will eventually make a hole in it. Similarly, you will wear down your opposition if you are tenacious. You will demonstrate persistence by not taking No for an answer. Keep wearing down your opponent with

comments like "Yes, but . . ." or "When else could we meet?" or "Let's keep trying till we do find a way."

- **Competition.** Let people know that you have choices. They will feel less secure knowing that your needs can be satisfied elsewhere. So you can say, "If you can't, then I will ask ____" or "I can get more from ____."

- **Knowledge.** Let people know about your expertise. Show them your qualifications (legitimacy). The more impressed they are with your credentials, the easier it will be to influence them. Also, demonstrate your knowledge with facts and examples of where you have been successful before (precedent).

- **Rationality.** Give people the data to back up your opinions. Presenting the data in writing (legitimacy) will further increase your power.

- **Rank.** You can rank positively or negatively. If people think that you will make a decision irrespective of their opinions, because your rank allows you to, they will find ways of subverting the implementation. So if you use rank, do so only as a last resort, reminding people only momentarily of your position. You can also increase your power by linking yourself with people who have a higher rank. For example, say, "The president told me that . . ."

Using Win-Win Tactics

*Don't ever slam a door; you might want to
go back.*

DON HEROLD (1889–1966),
AUTHOR AND HUMORIST

Nobody likes to lose. This is especially true in the business
world, where failure might mean a loss of career and income.
To ensure that your team works co-operatively and without detri-
mental competition (as opposed to beneficial competition, such as
that between ideas), master these win-win tactics:

Before You Negotiate
- Prepare yourself thoroughly and evaluate all the pertinent information available about the issue. Bring notes into the
  negotiations if you are not confident of remembering all the key
  points.
- Make a list of all plausible outcomes. Figure out which one will
  best benefit you and your team, and which might be considered
  acceptable fall-back positions. Decide how you might counter the
  other outcomes, and add these ideas to your notes.

When You Begin
- Determine or establish (depending on with whom you are
  negotiating, and what your position at the table is) a joint goal,
  however broad. This will foster an atmosphere of agreement, as
  opposed to antagonism.
- Set some ground rules — these can include not interrupting,

listening with respect, focusing on facts rather than personalities, and so on.

- State your position and needs clearly. Use "I" statements and bias-free language.
- Ask the other parties to make similar statements, and listen carefully, asking questions when you are not sure you understand.

As You Negotiate

- Establish common ground and common interests, and use them as the basis for a solution.
- Always explain your decision to decline a proposal.
- Be assertive, not aggressive (see Assertiveness, page 17).
- Don't place blame — it is counter-productive and poisons the negotiating atmosphere.
- Keep discussions on track and as brief as possible.
- Deal with the present and the future, not the past.
- Paraphrase and summarize to make sure you are understanding properly.
- Prioritize issues in terms of flexibility (is a point negotiable or firm?) and time constraint (does this point need to be resolved right now?). Agreeing to small things will make it easier to effect a compromise on larger issues.
- Realize that deadlines will force people to concede more as they loom nearer. Don't reveal your deadline, if you have one.
- Take occasional breaks to ask how everyone is feeling about the progress so far.
- Try for creative solutions that incorporate common goals and interests, and are not zero-sum.
- Use positive verbal and body language. Smile often. Appear relaxed and open. (See Reading Body Language, page 54.)
- Use all your power to increase your ability to be persuasive (see Negotiating — Power Strategies, page 30).
- In a unionized environment, do not negotiate single items of

the collective agreement one on one. Go through the proper channels.

At the End

- Write down the agreed-upon terms. Circulate them to every person concerned in the negotiations.
- Don't give more than you have to out of relief at having reached a compromise.

Problem Solving

*Part of my job is to keep a vague sense of
unease throughout the entire company. The
minute you say the job is done, you're dead.*

ARTHUR MARTINEZ, CEO,
SEARS ROEBUCK & CO. MERCHANDISING GROUP

Inefficiency in most companies is caused by continually re-"solving" the same problem. Here are five simple hints to turn your team's problems into opportunities — or make them disappear for good.

1. Prioritize!
- Pick the most important issues first. Start with those causing the most customer complaints, greatest costs or most conflict.
- Address problems in your own backyard before you go on the hunt for other people's problems.
- Tackle the problems you have control over before breaking your teeth on the ones whose circumstances are beyond your control.

2. Break down problems.
- Disassemble a problem into its components and find solutions for each issue. Start with the largest first, and continue systematically through the issues until you are done — or the remaining issues are too small and petty to warrant any further attention.
- Establish a process for solving problems. A good one is: Define, Find the Cause, Find Solutions, Plan, Implement, Monitor. Post this in a prominent place and encourage your team members

to use it every time they're confronted with a problem. Always remember that solutions come after analysis, not before.

3. Get the facts.

- Problems often result from missing information. Find the facts about each of your problem's components, and you will probably find a solution much more easily.
- If the problem is well known and requires a quick solution, consider asking opinions of the people involved.
- Ensure that you have determined the root cause of the problem *before* you get to the solution.
- Understand your problem clearly by defining it in terms of the 5 Ws and an H: the What, Where, When, Who, Why and How of the problem.

4. Involve 'em all.

- The more people involved in finding the solution to a problem, the more people will be committed to implementing it.
- Add as many people as possible and practical to spread the workload. More people = Less work.
- Different colleagues bring different skills to problem solving — the more skill sets you can throw at a problem, the more creative solutions you will come up with. Ask new employees to be involved in the problem-solving process. They will not be bound by the "company paradigm" and will often offer unexpected and novel solutions.
- Forge a consensus decision so that all participants buy in to the solution.

5. Do the new.

- Aim for creative, original solutions to problems. Brainstorm with the entire team.
- Encourage wacky suggestions — often they contain the germ of the solution.

Personal Goal Setting

You've removed most of the roadblocks to success when you've learned the difference between motion and direction.

BILL COPELAND

Imagine going hiking in the bush without a compass or a map. Sure, it's fun for a while — you feel adventurous and daring — but, sooner or later, you will get lost. Now imagine pursuing your career without clearly articulated goals. What should your goals be, and how should you go about getting them?

Your goals are you.

- Goals are compatible with your beliefs, and in return define you.
- In the same way you place your mirror so you can check your appearance before going to work, put your goals in a visible place so you can check them every morning.
- If you look at your goals every day, you will soon notice if one of them seems a bit off. This may happen because your values have slowly shifted.
- Goals should also be prioritized around your values; if you enjoy volunteer work at a homeless shelter, arrange your schedule so that you work less overtime.
- Goals can be short-, medium- or long-term projects. The more immediate the goal, the more disciplined one needs to be to get it done.
- Break down a long-term goal into yearly, monthly or daily steps — earning a million dollars before you reach a given age is much

easier to achieve when you know what each month's contribution should be.

Make yourself accountable.

- Tell everybody what your goals are. The more people you tell, the more you will be reminded of them.
- Arrange a mutual watchdog plan: help someone else stick to his goals, while he keeps you to yours.

Be SMART.

Use this simple formula to articulate your goals:

- **S** is for specific: give a number or a name to your goal. If you want to be senior vice-president of marketing in five years, say that, rather than "I want to make senior-level management at some point."
- **M** is for measurable: this goes with specific. You shouldn't be able to fudge whether you succeeded or failed; if you put a number to your goal, you'll know.
- **A** is for agreed-upon: be willing to negotiate the goal if others are involved. Their input will lead to additional commitment.
- **R** is for realistic: don't plan to be the head of the NATO if you're not going to join the army.
- **T** is for time-based: break the goals down into time-bits, and measure what you've achieved in each time-bit. The best way to have a measurable goal is to give yourself a final deadline, then break down the goal into smaller time-based steps.

Time Management

*Time is nature's way of keeping everything
from happening at once.*

ANONYMOUS

*M*anaging time effectively will enable you to balance work and
personal life. It will reduce stress and improve your health.
Above all it will improve your career since you will spend more time
satisfying your internal and external customers.

Time is a precious commodity because it is a nonrenewable
resource. If used poorly or inappropriately, it cannot be recovered.
Furthermore, time wasting causes unnecessary stress, can lead to
missed deadlines and can result in poor client service. Here are some
practical ideas that will help you manage your time more effectively:

Getting Started
- Visit your office over a weekend and clean house:
  - ✓ Throw away miscellaneous pieces of paper such as Post-it
    Notes.
  - ✓ Record all your information in one system.
  - ✓ Improve your filing system.
  - ✓ Put things where you can gain access to information quickly
    and easily.
- Analyze how you spend your time. Use labels: A for time spent
  serving a customer (internal or external); B for time spent on
  tasks helping someone who is helping a customer; C for time
  spent on activities that do not benefit customers directly or
  indirectly (often fun). Record your time spent doing A, B and C
  activities over a couple of typical days. Categorize the time.

Analyze how much of your time was wasted and make note of the circumstances under which this occurred.

- Develop a plan to reduce B activities. Write down the plan. Commit to implementation. Consult the plan often.
- Plan the occasional C activity. Having fun and doing the things you enjoy should be done to preserve your sanity! But don't get too caught up in those activities lest they interfere with the A items.
- Invest in a time management system — manual or computerized — to give you a structure to work with.

Daily

- Start each day with a list of all the activities you wish to accomplish.
- Next, categorize and prioritize each activity as A or B activities. A activities are those that if not done will either adversely affect your reputation or negatively affect your customer service. Any others are B's.
- Plan to do all A activities first. However, avoid committing more than 70% of your day to A activities since unforeseen problems will invariably upset your plans and use up unavailable time.
- Allocate B items to other dates in your calendar, not necessarily the next day.
- Keep your daily checklist handy at all times. The list will have little value if you are constantly searching for it.
- Keep your desk clean. Put things where you can find them.
- Use your travel time effectively. Most planes and trains now have phones, and you can use your laptop computer with little interruption.
- Your car can be turned into an education centre where you listen to management audio-cassettes. Challenge yourself to write down the highlights of a cassette while you are enjoying your first morning coffee.

- Avoid meetings that are not critical. If your sole purpose for going to a meeting is to get information, you can get it from the minutes.
- Delegate your routine work to associates so that you can tackle planning, problems and challenging tasks (see Delegating, page 143).
- Do only one thing at a time, and complete it before taking on the next task.
- Get those you work with to respect your quiet time, time when you are planning the day's activities (first hour) or cleaning your desk at the end of the day.
- Avoid procrastination. Identify and deal with the source of your discomfort. The longer you procrastinate, the higher your stress level.
- Do less pleasant but important items first. You will gain a sense of relief and achievement.

Paperwork

- Keep your desk clean. Put things where you can find them. Don't put documents in temporary places.
- Deal with each piece of paper once. File it, respond to it or dump it.
- Reduce time by responding to correspondence in writing on the letter. Fax it back, or photocopy it and send it back to the sender.

Avoiding Time Wasters

Procrastination is the thief of time.

EDWARD YOUNG (1683–1765),

ENGLISH POET AND DRAMATIST

No one is perfect. Everyone wastes some time. The three activities that waste the most time are long meetings, interruptions and telephone calls. Here is how you can reduce each dramatically:

Meetings

- Avoid setting or attending unnecessary meetings.
- Prepare a detailed agenda (see Setting an Agenda, page 112).
- Get someone to monitor time and to inform participants if they are falling behind schedule.
- At the start of the meeting obtain agreement on the objective(s) to keep a focus and avoid time-consuming discussions on unrelated topics.
- Record ideas on a flipchart to reduce repetition.
- Avoid dealing with items not on the agenda. If someone goes off on a tangent,
  - ✓ politely ask what the matter has to do with the agreed-upon objective
  - ✓ ask if the item can be dealt with later or outside the meeting
  - ✓ put the item in a "Parking Lot" (recorded on a separate flipchart) to be dealt with at an agreed-upon time

Office Interruptions

- Stand when a colleague comes in to chat. This will prevent her from getting comfortable.

- Ask him if it's important.
- Ask her if you can talk later in her office, a place where you can control the length of the conversation.
- Walk out long enough to get him out of your office and then sneak back to continue your work.
- Close your door.

Telephone Calls

- Leave complete messages for people who are not available so they won't have to call back.
- Install a voice-mail system.
- Return calls to people's voice mail after business hours.
- Train your associates to deal with routine issues on your behalf and to screen your calls when you are under pressure.
- Avoid unnecessary chitchat by answering with your name followed by a question such as "How may I help you?"
- Increase your chances of speaking to someone after you are told that the person is "away from her desk" or "in a meeting" by asking
  - ✓ Can he be paged?
  - ✓ Could you find her for me?
  - ✓ Can he be interrupted?

  or say
  - ✓ I'm returning her call, which was important.

PART II

Communication

Communicating Upwards

The most important sale in life is to sell yourself to yourself.

MAXWELL MALTZ, AUTHOR OF *PSYCHO-CYBERNETICS*

Communicating effectively with those who have a higher rank is not only an important part of your job, it is also important for your career.

- Always keep your boss informed, particularly if a problem is looming. Bosses want to be prepared. They want to look good and in control. Embarrassing yours will come back to haunt you.
- Do not delay bad news. The grapevine will get to your boss before you do, robbing you of the opportunity to put your own slant on the issue.
- Make an appointment to meet with your boss when the issue becomes pressing. When doing so, state your objective and the time needed to cover the subject.
- Let management know the impact and importance of your information and advice.
- When presenting information have backup material available. Written documentation will strengthen your ability to influence.
- Present your ideas concisely and clearly.
- Be confident of your facts and opinions. Speak with a firm voice. Your body language should reinforce your confidence; lean forward and maintain eye contact on critical issues.
- Focus on solutions rather than problems. Anyone can highlight problems. Show that you not only have the answers but are willing to take responsibility to resolve them.

- Choose your words with care. For example, saying "To be honest with you" might suggest that you have not been honest to this point. Avoid exaggeration. Say, "I have important information for you" rather than "I have terrible news for you."
- When you think your boss is being unreasonable, do not respond with anger or avoidance. Cool down, explain how you feel and why. And always use *I*, not *you*. For example, "I don't think it's right" will go over a lot better than "You are wrong."
- If your boss criticizes you, learn from the feedback. If the feedback is not specific, ask how your boss would deal with the same situation.
- If you are unsure about how receptive your boss will be to an important new idea, run it by her in writing first. This will enable you to
  ✓ deal comprehensively with the issue
  ✓ give your boss time to review your proposal
- Follow the chain of command. Don't intentionally go around your boss. If you do, keep your boss informed.

Communicating with Associates

A well-informed employee is the best sales person a company can have.

E.J. Thomas, late chairman and CEO,
Goodyear Tire & Rubber Co.

*E*mployees value the opportunity to influence their companies, to have their voices heard and see changes as a result of their input. Here is how you can encourage upward communication:

- Encourage communication. Manage by walking around. Be visible. Make it easy for associates to meet with you. Maintain an open-door policy.
- Listen to what associates are telling you. Listen to understand rather than to rebut. Listen to thoughts as well as feelings.
- Ask for associates' opinions. This gesture makes employees feel valued and can have a positive impact on their commitment.
- Encourage associates' ideas by setting up suggestion systems, performance improvement teams, focus groups and communication sessions.
- Act on these ideas, to encourage involvement. If you can't act, explain as soon as possible.
- Thank associates for their suggestions, even if you don't always agree with them. Challenge yourself to think how the idea could work rather than why it may not.
- Try the smaller ideas. What associates could learn from a mistake will probably more than pay for the cost of a small failure.
- Communicate in simple language. Don't confuse people by using vocabulary they are unlikely to understand.

- Demonstrate respect for your associates by showing interest in their ideas, listening to them and encouraging their input.
- If you are not quite sure of an idea you are listening to, repeat it in your own words. This will reinforce your understanding and demonstrate your interest.
- Don't just tell your associates what to do, tell them why.
- Choose your words carefully. Associates may react strongly to words that put them down.
- Give bad news in private; one-on-one meetings (preferably in an informal atmosphere) make things appear less severe. In addition, such meetings provide an opportunity for your associate to vent frustrations, and they enhance problem solving.
- Be conscious of your communication *style*. You will discourage communication if you
    - ✓ **preach**. Talking in moralizing terms implies that others don't have the same or equal ethical standards.
    - ✓ **patronize**. It makes them feel like they are being treated like children.
    - ✓ **scold**. Waving your finger at someone makes that person feel inferior. Focus on the behaviour or problem.
    - ✓ **are negative**. Don't prejudice ideas. Look for the positive. If you always show your associates what's wrong with their suggestions, they soon stop giving them.
- Maintain a positive approach. Smile. Look and act interested.
- Don't try to become popular with your associates by criticizing your boss. You can't develop trust if you can't be trusted.
- Don't voice disagreement with your boss's instructions to your associates. Voice them to your boss.
- If your associates are angry,
    - ✓ don't get into an argument. It will escalate the problem.
    - ✓ listen to them without interruption. Allowing them to let off steam will solve half the problem.
    - ✓ recognize their right to feel angry.
    - ✓ ask them for ideas on how to solve the problem.

Oral Communication

Sticks and stones may break our bones, but words will break our hearts.

ROBERT FULGHUM, AUTHOR OF *ALL I REALLY NEED TO KNOW I LEARNED IN KINDERGARTEN*

No matter how many technological innovations for communication are invented, human beings will continue to have conversations to impart information. Given how long humans have been conversing, it is surprising that many people have difficulty communicating orally in a business environment. This is especially true when the conversation is between a manager and an employee. A good manager will learn how to keep the conversation ongoing, and the lines of communication open.

Open the door.
- Create an environment that encourages people to speak to you.
- Keep your office door open. Encourage your staff to approach you at any time without the need to make an appointment.
- Stroll around and speak to people casually.
- Make an effort to learn something about each of your staff members (children's names, favourite pet, etc.) and ask about these things, following up on previous conversations wherever possible (see Communicating with Associates, page 49).

Pick your moment.
- Don't have the conversation in a noisy area.
- Find a time when no one is under a time constraint or has an imminent deadline.

- Don't do work or answer phone calls during the conversation.
- Turn your pager and cell phone off.

Animate your conversations.

- Be specific and clear about what you want to discuss.
- Choose your words carefully — use "and" instead of "but" as a connector between sentences, "I" statements rather than "you" statements.
- Use bias-free language.
- Vary your tone and delivery to emphasize certain points and to keep people interested. For important points, lean forward, open your eyes wider and enunciate.
- Start off the conversation on a positive note, especially if the issue at hand is controversial.
- Be brief but interesting (you can use humour or an anecdote to draw people in).

Listen.

- Don't interrupt, finish other people's sentences or go on the defensive before someone has finished speaking.
- Treat the other people in the conversation with respect, and encourage them to participate.
- Be empathetic — if you can't agree with the substance of what someone is saying, try to understand and agree with his or her motivation for saying it.
- Listen with your eyes (see Reading Body Language, page 54).

Wrap it up.

- Get confirmation on specific commitments ("It will be done on Friday at 3:00 p.m." rather than "We'll get it done sometime before the end of the week").
- Paraphrase and summarize the main points of the conversation to make sure everyone else understands what has been said.

Crossing Language Barriers

O ur workforce is becoming more diverse. Communicating with people for whom English is a new language is critical.

- Be patient. If you expect too much, too quickly, you will confuse and frustrate.
- Don't show anger if people don't understand at first.
- If people speak English poorly, but understand reasonably well, ask them to demonstrate their understanding through actions rather than words.
- Avoid jokes. Your humour will not be understood. Worse still, it might be seen as a joke at their expense.
- Don't assume that difficulty in understanding means lack of intelligence. Many people doing menial jobs in their adopted country were teachers, engineers, lawyers and medical practitioners in their native countries.
- Speak slowly and clearly, but don't raise your voice.
- Use face-to-face communication whenever possible. Avoid telephone conversations.
- Break instructions into manageable steps.
- Use interpreters only if communications are impossible. Discourage people from becoming dependent on interpreters.
- Use pictures and diagrams instead of words. Back up oral directions with simple written instructions.
- Encourage people to take English courses. Make time available for them to get to classes.

Reading Body Language

*The most important thing in communicating is
to hear what isn't being said.*

PETER F. DRUCKER, MANAGEMENT
CONSULTANT AND UNIVERSITY PROFESSOR

*R*eading body language teaches you to listen with your eyes as
well as your ears. Here are a few common indicators in Western
culture — but keep in mind that other cultures have different
signals. Get a colleague from that culture to teach them to you.

BEHAVIOUR	LIKELY MEANING
Arms or legs crossed	Closed to your ideas, unreceptive
Body: leaning back	Skeptical, unwilling to commit
Body: leaning back with hands behind head	Relaxed, possible reservations, no sense of urgency
Body: leaning forward	Positive interest in topic
Body: slouching	Trying to be unobtrusive, low self-esteem
Eyes blinking slowly	Uncomfortable, unwilling to be there
Eyes at top left	Quickly evaluating and planning next manoeuvres — possibly hostile
Eyes at top right	Doing mental problem solving, trying to figure something out

BEHAVIOUR (cont.)	LIKELY MEANING (cont.)
Eyes darting	Anxious, unconfident, unprepared
Eyes looking over tops of glasses	Evaluating, assessing
Eyes narrowed	Evaluating, assessing, with possible skepticism
Eyes staring	Not paying attention, daydreaming
Eyes wide	Interested, making an important point
Hands at sides	Neutral
Hands clasped in back	Acknowledging authority, possibly something to hide
Hands clasped in front	Possibly conservative, closed mind
Hands on hips/hip jut	Confident, bordering on arrogant — issuing a challenge
Hands on table	Willing to get things done
Hands open, palms down	Demanding — showing control
Hands open, palms up	Asking, wanting, needing — showing vulnerability
Head cocked to one side	Listening with interest
Head straight on	Confident
Head tilted back	Arrogant, cocky
Head tilted down	Shy, ashamed or lying
Jacket buttoned	Formal
Jacket unbuttoned	Informal
Smile with eyes crinkled	Joyful, expressing pleasure
Smile without eyes crinkled	Trying to gain approval

Managing the Grapevine

Surveys show that most people get the information they need through the grapevine rather than official channels. Here's what you can do to reduce the impact of distorted information:

Avoid rumours.

- Take the attitude that it is better to give too much information than too little.
- Hold regular briefings, which by definition should be short. They can be stand-up meetings in the office or a huddle on the factory floor. If you don't have new information, encourage questions, which may uncover rumours you are not aware of.
- Keep a flipchart in your work area. Write news on it regularly. Allow your people to record questions that they want to deal with at your meetings.
- Anticipate issues that might provoke negative gossip. Deal with them right away.

Deal with rumours.

- Never deny or lie about the truth — your credibility will suffer and trust between you and your people will be jeopardized. Often information reaches your people before you get it. Try to track down the source and establish whether the information is truth or fiction. When you have the facts, let people have them right away.
- Go to the source of the rumour. Find out if you or your team will be affected. Find ways to position yourself to take advantage of the situation. Develop a plan that will demonstrate how you and your people could help to make the change successful.

- When you go to the source of a rumour, don't demand answers or put people on the spot. Make it easy for them to help you by asking questions that can be dealt with hypothetically. For example: "If, at some time in the future, there was a downsizing, which departments would be cut first?" Watch their body language when they answer in order to understand how they feel about the issue.
- Maintain a positive attitude. Take particular care to do good work, since deteriorating attitude and work will make you stick out like a sore thumb.
- Be open to change. Look at all the alternatives. Change brings opportunities. New directions should challenge and energize you.
- Watch for signs that rumours are becoming reality. Typically, senior managers will be
  - ✓ spending more time in meetings
  - ✓ looking harassed
  - ✓ whispering among themselves
  - ✓ taking phone calls or holding discussions behind closed doors

Written Communication

Writing without thinking is like shooting without aiming.

ARNOLD H. GLASGOW

Written communication is a basic business skill, but unfortunately one with which many people feel uncomfortable. Writing skills will only improve with practice, but here are a few pointers to jump-start you on the road to effective written communication:

Should you write?

Some ideas are best expressed verbally or visually. Written communications are most effective when they address an important or complex decision over which a lot of time and thought must be expended.

Keep it simple.
- Order your material in a logical point-form sequence before you begin. Make sure to cover 4 Ws and an H: Who, What, When, Where and How.
- Write conversationally, in the way you would speak to team members.
- Send copies only to colleagues who are directly concerned.

Keep it short.
- Use plain language wherever possible, and highlight key terms and ideas using formatting and context rather than repetition.

- Short sentences and short paragraphs will make reading easier and will draw your target audience into the meat of your communication.
- Attach additional details and documents at the end as appendices rather than including them in the main text.

Keep it positive.

- State up front the advantage of reading your note ("This plan will increase team efficiency by 75%").
- Accentuate the positive aspects of your proposal.
- Shape your writing to reflect your understanding of your readers' needs by using lots of "you" statements.
- Employ bias-free language at all times — use plural subjects, neutral or plural pronouns and nouns and avoid possessives.

Keep practising.

- Read your work aloud, making changes until you feel it works.
- Keep copies of written work that you find particularly effective, and refer to them often.

E-mail

E-mail has become the most effective form of business communication. E-mail can be sent around the world, instantly, to as many people as you wish at any time of day or night. But some people are still a bit uncomfortable with e-mail technology, and others fail to treat e-mail and e-mail writing as seriously as "hardcopy" written communication. Here are some tips that will help make e-mail as easy and as effective as you want it to be.

Be efficient.
- E-mail is a fast medium — don't let your messages fester in your in-folder. Respond to business e-mail within the same business day or, better yet, right after you receive it.
- Don't send huge sound or picture files as attachments unless you can compress them —the download time will annoy your recipients. Don't send huge attachments at all to people with personal-use Internet providers, which often have limits on file size — your e-mail may be bounced back.

Keep it simple.
- Keep your messages brief and to the point.
- Space paragraphs clearly, since many servers reformat outside e-mails.
- If you need a lot of text space to convey your message, write a short note and send the details as an attachment.
- If you are responding to specific sections of an e-mail, include only those sections in your response, rather than sending back the whole letter.

Learn to send and receive e-mail effectively.

- Always include a pithy and concise title in the subject line.
- Use the "cc" box to copy the e-mail to other interested parties. However, if you wish the original recipient(s) to be unaware that others are also receiving the e-mail, copy it using the "bcc" box.
- If you regularly send out identical e-mails to the same group of people, put them on a listserv. Be careful not to send an e-mail to the listserv that is intended for only one person on it.
- Keep a hard copy of important e-mail correspondence.
- Some programs will let you filter unwanted or low-priority (usually personal) e-mail. Use this feature if your e-mail volume is high.

Communicate clearly.

(See also Written Communication, page 58.)

- Use more paragraphs than you would in an ordinary letter — it is more difficult to read type on screen than on paper, and the more white space you provide, the more likely it is that your message will be understood.
- Proofread your messages for spelling and grammatical errors.
- Reread your messages before pressing Send. Because of the speed at which e-mail is often composed, and because e-mail is seen as more conversational than a formal business letter, people are often not as careful with tone as they are in a more formal letter. And tone can be easily misinterpreted by the recipient, often to your detriment. Always make sure that your tone conveys what you intended it to.

Know your e-mail etiquette.

- Don't shout (avoid using all capital letters).
- Know that e-mail is not a private medium; messages you send to one party may be forwarded to others. Be circumspect in your language and humour.

- Be careful what you forward, and to whom. Just because it's written down doesn't mean it's true! In the case of virus warnings, bookmark a web site (www.symantec.com is a good one) so that you can check the reliability of the warning before forwarding it.

The Internet

Just because everything is different doesn't mean anything has changed.

IRENE PETER, U.S. WRITER

*T*he Internet: it's here to stay. So harness its power and put it to work for you. The most surprising thing about the Net is that it takes very little computer savvy to get started; as those before you have done, you will learn as you go.

Here are some rules to surf by:

- Never give up. If you have trouble finding specific information, persevere. It's invariably on the Web somewhere, and only waits to be uncovered. Streamline your search as much as possible and follow search tips suggested by various search engines.
- Don't assume that just because it's on the Net, it's true! Any person or group can set up a web site and begin handing out advice. Always confirm what you read by consulting several sources.
- Familiarity breeds reliability. Only download software from respectable sites. Whenever possible, select web sites that are produced by people or organizations you already trust.
- Respect the copyright of printed material you extract from the Net and be aware of any legal limits that apply to files you download. Files that are in the public domain, such as the works of Hemingway, have no restrictions. Freeware and shareware files are copyrighted, but require little or no fee for use.
- Be security-smart. The information you send on the Net goes through many different public networks, meaning that lots of

people have access to it. But what about when you want info, such as your credit card number, to remain private? To protect your information you can use specific security tools, such as encryption, which makes the information you send unreadable while in transit. Only the designated recipient, who has the software to decrypt the information, can read it. Other software tools that enhance Internet security are also available.

- Change your password regularly, avoiding obvious words that hackers will try first.

- Never divulge your real address or phone number in a public forum or message base.

- Be selective about to whom you choose to give access to your Net account.

- Safeguard against viruses. Viruses are an unfortunate fact of life on the Net. There are new ones emerging every day and software is constantly in development to combat them. Ensure that you have downloaded the latest anti-virus software from your server. And never open any e-mail messages that are unfamiliar to you, or suspicious in nature; simply delete them.

- Closely compare Internet service providers. Service levels and offerings vary greatly here, and the various companies are highly competitive. Ask your friends and colleagues about their experiences and which ones they recommend.

- Familiarize yourself with all the Net has to offer. Become a confident surfer. But be warned: surfing can be highly addictive. Check out all the associations and organizations related to your field, subscribe to newsgroups, ask others online for their suggestions. Get your name on their electronic mailing lists. Join your peers in chat rooms and discussion groups. Share ideas and e-mail addresses. Download helpful book and magazine excerpts.

- Use the Net to help keep you on top of your world, professionally and personally.

Report Writing

Lay down the most complicated movements intelligibly, but in a few words with simplicity.

NAPOLEON BONAPARTE (1769–1821)

Report writing is a critical skill as you move up the corporate ladder. Here are some ideas about how to do it effectively:

- Be clear about the goal of your report. Exclude any information that will detract from your objective.
- Know your audience:
  - ✓ Imagine what they want to find in the report.
  - ✓ Anticipate and cover their objections.
- Be a storyteller:
  - ✓ Start by grabbing the reader's attention with a challenge.
  - ✓ Maintain interest with an absorbing middle.
  - ✓ Reward the reader with a memorable ending.
- Use simple language. Don't confuse people or try to impress them with words seldom used.
- Be brief. Cut out any words that do not make a sentence clearer or more concise.
- Avoid phrases or words that can cause confusion, including
  - ✓ slang — "hit the bricks"
  - ✓ jargon — "this task is really Mickey Mouse"
  - ✓ clichés — "when hell freezes over"
- Make the report believable:
  - ✓ Avoid generalizations.
  - ✓ Don't exaggerate.
  - ✓ Avoid exclusionary language.

- Address readers as if you're talking to them.
- Maintain an upbeat, positive tone.
- Simplify your sentences. Ask yourself after each sentence and paragraph, "Is there an easier way of expressing what I have written?"
- Use bullets to list points.
- Use headings and subheadings wherever possible to allow the reader to scan the report and grasp key concepts.
- Keep paragraphs as short as possible. Divide paragraphs that are more than 10 lines long.
- Use as much white space as possible to create a user-friendly site.
- Start a new sentence for each thought. Avoid using "and" or "but."

REPORT WRITING CHECKLIST

Evaluate your report against these criteria before it is distributed.

	Yes	No
• Is the tone right? (Is it not too antagonistic or condescending?)	❏	❏
• Is the style right? (Is it too formal, informal or the right mix?)	❏	❏
• Is it organized well? (Does it flow? Is its order logical?)	❏	❏
• Is the message clear? (Do you get to the point quickly? Are key issues the focus?)	❏	❏
• Is the report interesting to read? (Is the writing style challenging and interesting?)	❏	❏
• Is the vocabulary simple? (Is the report easy to read? Is it free of jargon?)	❏	❏
• Does sentence structure make it easy to read? (Are sentences short? Have you avoided joining two thoughts using "and" or "but"?)	❏	❏

Amend your report if you have any No responses.

REPORT WRITING ROADMAP

STEP 1
Define your purpose.

STEP 2
Define your audience.

STEP 3
Create preliminary statements of purpose and content.

STEP 4
Gather data.

STEP 5
Organize ideas for writing. Collect core sentences on cue cards.

STEP 6
Write a rough draft (nonstop).

STEP 7
Edit. Add visuals.

STEP 8
Write final draft.

Speeches

One thing a speaker should remember for sure; the mind can absorb only what the seat can endure.

UNKNOWN

*M*aking a speech is one of the most difficult and intimidating tasks. These ideas will make the process a lot easier.

Preparing for the Speech

- Accept only invitations with adequate lead times. If you don't have time to prepare and rehearse, decline.
- Learn as much as you can about your audience. Find out about their
  - ✓ age
  - ✓ sex
  - ✓ background
  - ✓ education
- Establish an objective, something you will say at the end to make the speech memorable. Work backwards to craft your speech.
- Draw a mental map of what you want to get across to your audience. For example, a talk about leadership may have a model such as the one shown below:

courage   vision   reality   ethics

- Develop an outline of key points.
- Order your points so that there is a natural flow of ideas.
- Establish sub-points under each key item.
- Record your information on 3-by-5-inch cue cards as reminders or prompts. Use one card per key point.
- Don't write out your speech word for word. Reading it will bore your audience and make you speak in a monotone, which will increase your discomfort since this is not your usual manner of speaking.
- Practise until you are confident. Your dry run can be done
  - ✓ in front of a mirror
  - ✓ into a tape recorder
  - ✓ in front of an mentor
  - ✓ on video
- Avoid body language that projects insincerity, nervousness or unhappiness. Watch TV programs where interviewees are drilled by experienced investigative reporters to learn how to recognize and avoid negative mannerisms.
- Establish some good closing remarks that will summarize your key thoughts and leave the audience uplifted.
- Visualize yourself making the speech with confidence. Imagining your success will become a self-fulfilling prophecy.
- Remember the three secrets of high-impact presentations:
  - ✓ Be sincere.
  - ✓ Be quick.
  - ✓ Be seated.

Making the Speech

- Dress for the occasion. If you are unsure of your audience, dress up rather than too casually. Dress conservatively for most business situations.
- Grab the attention of your audience:
  - ✓ Challenge your audience by starting off with one of the 5 Ws and an H: Who would like . . . ? What would be the one . . . ?

When was the last time you . . .? Where is the best place you . . .? Why is it that . . .? How can you . . .?

✓ Quote a shocking statistic or take a controversial stance.

✓ Start with humour, but only if you are good at telling jokes, and only if the story is relevant to the subject. Avoid jokes that could offend. The best humour is a story that is self-deprecating. Not only will such a story amuse your audience, but it will develop a link with them since you are signalling to them that you are "normal."

- Project positive body language:

  ✓ Stand erect and tall. Push your chest out. A positive body posture will project confidence and make you feel good.

  ✓ Avoid putting your hands on one or both hips. Hands on both hips will separate you from the audience since it projects arrogance. A protrusion of one hip signals that you don't want to be there.

  ✓ Maintain steady eye contact with your audience. Fast-shifting eyes indicate a lack of certainty.

- Use gestures to increase your effectiveness:

  ✓ Open your arms to the audience, when appropriate, as if to embrace them.

  ✓ Keep your arms at your sides when you are not using them.

  ✓ Keep arm gestures between your waist and shoulder.

  ✓ Avoid quick and jerky gestures since these give the impression of nervousness.

  ✓ Vary gestures to suit your message. A continuous single gesture will be distracting.

  ✓ Don't overuse gestures or they will lose their impact.

- Use as much of the space in front of your audience as possible. Avoid standing behind a lectern.

- Use simple language. Words with more than two syllables are more difficult to understand.

- Never use sexist language or say anything that belittles any ethnic or minority group. You will offend your audience.

- Create interest by involving your audience and changing your pace. For instance, take a poll or ask for opinions. Find out if anyone can relate to the example you have described. This interaction will show you are interested in, and care for, the opinion of your audience.
- Avoid going over material that is common knowledge. Your information should be news to the audience if you want to hold their attention.
- Keep your audience's attention and make your speech interesting:
  - ✓ Illustrate points with anecdotes and quotes.
  - ✓ Use props to add impact. Hold up articles, books or magazines when you quote from recognized experts.
  - ✓ Change your voice modulation. Speak quickly, slowly, loudly or softly for brief moments.
  - ✓ Pause before or after a key thought.
- Tell people what you are going to tell them, tell them and then tell them what you told them.
- Make sure your ending is as challenging as your introduction. Leave the audience with something to think about.

Avoiding Nervousness

The biggest fear of North Americans, greater even than death and snakes, is talking in front of others. Many a speech has been destroyed by anxiety. Here's what you can do to reduce your stress.

- Prepare thoroughly to improve confidence.
- Use cue cards. This will help you talk normally (with eye contact) and keep in touch with your audience.
- Be yourself. Emulating someone else will make you feel awkward and the audience will react with skepticism.
- Spend a few minutes alone before the presentation to collect your thoughts and focus your energy.
- Before you start, take a few deep breaths.
- Never admit you are nervous. Doing so will draw attention to the problem instead of your message.

- Maintain eye contact with a friendly face in the audience. Your confidence will increase. Similarly, avoid eye contact with someone who looks unhappy.
- Don't play with a pointer, pen, change in your pocket or anything else that may be handy. You will distract the audience. Empty your pockets before your speech.
- If you have a small audience, begin your presentation casually with a two-way discussion of something topical. This will reduce tension and allow you to ease into your speech.
- Visualize your audience in a non-threatening way, such as sitting on a throne or with their underwear on! They will appear less threatening.

Presentations

*Speeches are like babies – easy to conceive,
hard to deliver.*

PAT O'MALLEY

Y ou can have the best idea in the world, but if you can't sell it
your idea will die on the vine. Here's how to get ready for a
presentation and conduct it with maximum impact:

Preparation

- Learn all you can about your audience. Discover their hot
buttons.
- Prepare your presentation. Assemble appropriate supporting
documentation. If the presentation is complex, have a package of
information prepared for each participant (distribute in advance
if possible).
- Decide on the best medium for your presentation. The most
commonly used media are slides or overheads for a formal presentation, or flipcharts for an informal presentation. People
require about 40% less time to grasp a concept with visual aids
than with verbal instruction alone.
- Remember, your audience will access information in three ways:
    - ✓ visual
    - ✓ auditory
    - ✓ kinesthetic

Your presentation should include all three for maximum impact.

- Plan your agenda. It should cover
    - ✓ welcome and introductions
    - ✓ objectives

- ✓ the problem
- ✓ the solution
- ✓ the benefits
- ✓ your action plan
- ✓ how you arrived at your conclusion
- ✓ questions and answers
- ✓ request for go ahead
- ✓ wrap-up
- Prepare your slides or overheads:
  - ✓ Keep them short and to the point.
  - ✓ Use one idea per transparency or slide.
  - ✓ Add a picture where possible.
  - ✓ Make sure that letters are large, bold and legible.
- Plan your presentation to last no more than 15 to 20 minutes. For simpler proposals, shorter is better. Use the KISS principle (keep it short and simple).
- Assemble all your information and do a dry run out loud. Imagine the audience in front of you. Gauge their reaction. Record your presentation so that you can refine it and adjust timing.
- Assemble an emergency kit of markers, masking tape, name cards, spare bulbs, pencils and pens.
- Give people plenty of notice of your presentation. Confirm their attendance.

Set-up

- Get to the meeting room early. Make sure that the seating arrangement and equipment are as you requested.
- Check the view from several seats to ensure that everyone can see the overhead screen and the flipchart.
- Check all equipment. If you are using a slide or overhead projector, make sure that you know how it works and that it does work.
- Have spare bulbs handy. The more important the presentation, the greater the chance that something might go wrong — that's Murphy's Law.

- Prepare places for each person and provide writing paper and a pen if necessary. However, do not hand out your presentation at this time. People will tend to read your material instead of listening to you. Pass it out at the end of the presentation.

Conducting the Presentation

- Relax, and welcome people into the meeting room. Show your confidence and approachability with a firm handshake and a smile.
- When all are seated, welcome them officially and let them know what to expect. Remind them of your agenda, the expected outcome, the amount of time you intend to take and breaks. Tell them you will pass out copies of the presentation after you have finished. Also, let them know where the washrooms and fire exits are.
- Let people know if you intend to take questions as they occur or whether you prefer them at the end of the presentation. The former approach will show greater interest in the attendees and greater confidence in your ability.
- Follow your agenda step-by-step.
- Start off with as much impact as possible. Present a challenge or recall a story that will move your audience.
- Ask rhetorical questions from time to time. Challenge your audience. Conduct periodic polls by asking a question that needs a show of hands for an answer.
- When you conduct a question-and-answer session, focus on those people who are likely to be constructive and positive.
- If a question comes from someone who rambles a lot, you might say, "Can you summarize your ideas in about 20 words?"
- Paraphrase questions to give yourself time to formulate an answer. You will also give people who didn't hear the question a chance to do so.
- If you don't have an answer, say so. You can ask if others have an answer or offer to do some research and get back to them later.

- Use questions as a chance to reinforce key principles.
- Avoid letting hostile people destroy your presentation by
  - ✓ not being defensive
  - ✓ not engaging in verbal sparring
  - ✓ using humour to diffuse tension
  - ✓ providing facts rather than opinions
  - ✓ canvassing other opinions to show alternative approaches
  - ✓ offering to deal with their issues,
  - ✓ offering to deal with their issues outside the meeting if unrelated to your topic (see Problem Behaviour in Meetings, page 116)
- Keep the presentation short and to the point. Don't cover material that is already known to the audience. Focus on new information.
- Do not read word-for-word from your notes, slides or overheads. The audience can do that, too. Give people a chance to read each visual and then paraphrase the contents, stressing key points.
- Provide a bridging comment between overheads and slides so that your presentation is knitted together.
- Maintain eye contact with your audience:
  - ✓ Scan the audience, looking at each person for three to five seconds.
  - ✓ Don't read off the screen or turn your back on people.
- Keep people's attention by
  - ✓ changing the pace of presentation from time to time
  - ✓ doing something different at least every seven minutes: asking questions, polling the audience, having them complete a questionnaire, doing group work and so on
  - ✓ modulating your voice: speak loudly and then softly, quickly and then deliberately
  - ✓ animating your facial expressions and gestures
  - ✓ punching the air on key points
- Move around the room, getting closer to your audience when they ask questions. Staying behind a podium builds a wall between you and your audience.

PRESENTATION CHECKLIST

Use this list to evaluate your performance and identify things you might do differently next time.

	Yes	No
Did you . . .		
• thank participants for coming?	❏	❏
• show and follow an agenda?	❏	❏
• get agreement to length of meeting?	❏	❏
• show benefits early?	❏	❏
• use the KISS principle?	❏	❏
• avoid getting into small details?	❏	❏
• show confidence?	❏	❏
• use a variety of visual aids?	❏	❏
• avoid using notes?	❏	❏
• speak deliberately?	❏	❏
• use the floor space?	❏	❏
• have eye contact with the audience?	❏	❏
• give credit to those who helped?	❏	❏
• keep the presentation positive?	❏	❏
• ask for, not demand, support?	❏	❏
• involve members of your team?	❏	❏
• summarize?	❏	❏
• finish on time?	❏	❏

Using Visual Media in Presentations

*P*eople will remember information that is presented orally and visually far more than orally alone. Here is what you can do to enhance your visual presentations:

Using a Flipchart

- Write in bold, capital letters.
- Use dark colours for words — black or dark blue is best.
- Use colours for highlighting, underlining and bullets.
- Emphasize headings by writing them larger, using a different colour or underlining.
- Keep one idea per page. Use tape tabs so you can find prewritten pages quickly.
- Post key ideas on the walls for easy reference.
- Precut masking tape and stick pieces on the legs of the flipchart stand. Use them to post pages onto the walls.
- Avoid using markers made from strong chemicals. The writing may bleed through your flipchart paper.
- Use diagrams and flowcharts to increase understanding.
- Add pictures where possible. Remember, a picture is worth a thousand words!

Using Overheads or Slides

- Check that the light bulb is working. Some machines use two light bulbs in case one fails. Check both.
- Learn how to use the overhead beforehand. Different manufacturers have different switching systems.
- Focus the machine before you start to avoid the embarrassment of an indistinct picture.

- Clean the face plate to remove dirt that will project onto the screen.
- Number your transparencies and have them laid out in front of you so you can see the next one before you get to it. This will help you to "bridge" the information from one transparency to the next.
- Use the four-by-four rule. Try not to exceed four lines per transparency and avoid more than four words per line.
- Don't use your fingers to point to items on your transparency. Your hand might shake, making people aware of your nervousness. Use a stir stick or pencil (not a round one, as it will roll).
- Show all the information first, before showing each item individually.
- Make sure you don't block the audience's view of the visuals.

Using a Computerized System

- Use a machine that you are familiar with. These high-tech toys are sometimes made for computer gurus and not for us mere mortals.
- If you are using someone else's equipment, get there early to familiarize yourself with it. Ask someone who knows the equipment to be there to help you set up.
- Take a copy of your presentation on disk in case your laptop doesn't communicate with the LCD projector. You may be able to use an existing computer.
- If the equipment doesn't work the first time, before you call for help or break out into a sweat, ensure that
  - ✓ everything is plugged in
  - ✓ the computer and the LCD are connected
  - ✓ you have tried an alternative portal
  - ✓ you reboot your computer with the LCD still switched on
- Design your presentation using the same principles you would use for overheads (i.e., have one idea per slide).
- If you make a change in a PowerPoint presentation during a

break, be sure to save it before beginning again, or you run the risk of the presentation freezing.

- Turn the picture off when not needed by using the Pause button on the LCD or Control–B or –W on your computer.
- Stand back from the screen so that you can see the audience. Use an extended-cord mouse or, better still, a remote control device.
- Demonstrate that you are starting a new module by changing the background colour or changing to a new template.
- Use background noise or other gimmicks only as special effects for key ideas.

Teamwork

Team Building

Someone said that the membership of a club is made up of four kinds of bones.
There are WISHBONES, who spend their time wishing someone else would do the work.
There are JAWBONES, who do all the talking but little else.
Next come the KNUCKLEBONES, who knock everything that everyone else tried to do.
And finally, there are the BACKBONES, who get under the load and do the work.

ANONYMOUS

Doing some planning before a team is constituted will help you choose members wisely and keep the team running successfully.

Designing a Team

- Develop a mission. Teams need a purpose. They also need to know how they fit into the overall framework and strategy. They need to know why they are being set up and what they must accomplish.
- Clarify roles, boundaries and expectations. The clearer it is to team members how they will operate, the quicker they will get going and the fewer the conflicts.
- Plan to transfer responsibility. If the team is a permanent one, it should assume as much responsibility for its own management as possible. Develop a milestone chart to promote the orderly transfer of tasks to the team. Ensure a training plan is in place to make this happen effectively.

- Determine the best structure. Decide whether the team should be cross-functional or a collection of people doing similar tasks. This decision will be influenced by whether your organization needs to break down interdepartmental barriers or create commitment to a common goal.
- Understand the purpose of the team. Be clear about
  - ✓ what the team will be doing
  - ✓ whether it will be temporary or permanent
  - ✓ who your customers are
  - ✓ how you will measure success
  - ✓ what the pressures will be
  - ✓ what those you report to expect

Selecting Team Members

- Develop a profile sheet for each person and position on the team. Your description should include
  - ✓ previous experience on a team
  - ✓ previous work experience
  - ✓ technical skills required
  - ✓ communication skills
  - ✓ willingness to take responsibility
  - ✓ self-confidence
  - ✓ appropriate education
- Select the team leader. If possible, involve team members in the selection. An effective leader will be someone who
  - ✓ encourages participation
  - ✓ can listen
  - ✓ understands the corporate culture
  - ✓ is prepared to take risks
  - ✓ is able to give constructive feedback
  - ✓ understands team dynamics
  - ✓ enjoys promoting people
  - ✓ can maintain momentum
- Select team members. While 10 to 12 might be an ideal number,

teams as small as 5 or as large as 15 can work well, too. Select people with the necessary technical skills. Also look for people with the social and team skills to complement one another's personalities.

Starting

- Call a meeting. Explain the purpose of the team.
- Indicate what the goals are and how they will be measured.
- Establish the rewards for goal achievement.
- Share your strategy for improving performance with the team. If you don't have a strategy, ask for input. If you have one, ask for feedback.
- Spell out the benefits of participating on the team. If members see what's in it for them, they will be enthusiastic about other benefits.
- Negotiate the ground rules. Using a flipchart, identify key behaviours that will enable team members to work together in harmony. Confirm agreement to the rules. Post the ground rules in a prominent place to ensure that they are not forgotten
- Identify skills of team members to see how they complement each other.
- Meet regularly, formally or informally, to ensure that momentum does not stop.
- Celebrate successes, particularly those that are measurable. Celebrations increase cohesiveness and develop a sense of pride.
- Allow the team members to take on as much responsibility as they are willing to and are trained for. Increasing delegation of responsibility over time will increase ownership for performance among team members.
- Recruit people with complementary technical and social skills. There is strength in diversity. For example, a natural "devil's advocate" will challenge the group to search for more alternatives before making decisions, which will enhance creativity and the quality of decisions.

Teamwork

*I'm just a plowhand from Arkansas, but I have
learned how to hold a team together . . . how
to lift some men up, how to calm down others,
until they've got one heartbeat together . . .*

BEAR BRYANT (1913–83), LEGENDARY FOOTBALL COACH

*M*aintaining performance at a high level for the benefit of
your customers is essential. You can sustain and even improve
performance if you

- Measure critical indicators of your success such as
  - ✓ quality
  - ✓ timeliness
  - ✓ cost effectiveness
- Display these measures prominently so that people can track the
  impact of their efforts immediately.
- Set team, rather than individual, goals for key indicators.
- Provide regular feedback on team performance to members. Your
  feedback will build involvement and commitment, and a sense of
  pride as results improve.
- Celebrate improvements to promote a sense of pride and team
  cohesiveness. Celebrating can be as simple as a "thank you" at a
  spontaneous meeting on the shop floor or a luncheon off-site.
  Some teams develop their own ceremonies and symbols like ring-
  ing a bell when new records have been established. Encourage
  unique ways of celebrating, even though they will be out of character with the corporate culture.
- If performance declines, don't look for victims. Involve the team

in problem solving. Find out why performance has dropped and ask for ideas on how to improve.

- Develop action plans for improvement. Involve the team in this process. Develop a list of actions with specific dates for implementation. Ask team members to take responsibility.
- Set aside time for having fun at the beginning of a meeting, at the end of a day or outside working hours.
- Encourage the development of a team subculture. The group will develop its own ceremonies and symbols to promote its sense of being unique.
- Have high expectations of the team. Challenge people at all times. Let them know the extent of your confidence in them.
- Encourage job rotation, if your technology allows it. The benefits include
  - ✓ less monotony
  - ✓ learning new skills
  - ✓ personal growth
  - ✓ empathy for one another's problems
  - ✓ shared ownership of performance
  - ✓ improved productivity
  - ✓ less downtime
- Reward collaborative behaviour. Encourage team members to pitch in and help one another when workloads have become difficult for a few members of the team.
- Encourage people to get to know one another on a personal level, without unduly invading people's privacy.
- Involve the team in the decision to recruit new members.
- Recruit people with well-developed interpersonal skills. Knowing how to listen, give feedback and manage conflict are critical skills for effective team members.
- Establish ground rules. Allow members to monitor and deal with transgressors.
- Remove poor performers and continuously negative people. They will sap the energy of the team and cause dissension.

SURVEY TO MEASURE TEAM MORALE

This survey will establish what you like about the team and what you dislike. The data will be used to identify ongoing opportunities to enhance each member's satisfaction in the team.

Your best response is always what you really think. Avoiding difficult issues will prevent them from being dealt with openly and honestly.

Read the statements below and circle the responses that best reflect how you feel. 1 = strongly disagree; 2 = disagree; 3 = neither agree nor disagree; 4 = agree; 5 = strongly agree.

INVOLVEMENT

People on our team always feel included because we

1. share information openly	1	2	3	4	5
2. make decisions after including all opinions	1	2	3	4	5
3. do not work in cliques	1	2	3	4	5

CO-OPERATION

People work well together because we

1. pitch in and help one another	1	2	3	4	5
2. offer to help if someone is under pressure	1	2	3	4	5
3. try to make sure that workloads are evenly spread	1	2	3	4	5

COMMUNICATION

Communication in the team is effective because we

1. express ourselves openly and honestly	1	2	3	4	5
2. have no hidden agendas	1	2	3	4	5
3. don't discuss people behind their backs	1	2	3	4	5
4. give feedback to one another as needed	1	2	3	4	5

ORGANIZATION

Our team is well organized in that

1. our roles are clearly defined	1	2	3	4	5
2. goals are specific	1	2	3	4	5
3. responsibilities are clear	1	2	3	4	5
4. we use the talents of our people fully	1	2	3	4	5
5. we have productive meetings	1	2	3	4	5
6. tasks get done on time	1	2	3	4	5
7. our systems are effective	1	2	3	4	5

IMPROVEMENT

Our team gets better all the time because we

1. continuously improve our systems/methods	1	2	3	4	5
2. try new things	1	2	3	4	5
3. take risks	1	2	3	4	5
4. focus on the future, not on the past	1	2	3	4	5
5. are customer-driven	1	2	3	4	5
6. track our results and improvements	1	2	3	4	5
7. are able to learn new skills	1	2	3	4	5

ATMOSPHERE

It is great to be on the team because we

1. have a lot of fun	1	2	3	4	5
2. celebrate successes	1	2	3	4	5
3. treat each other as individuals, not employees	1	2	3	4	5
4. all have the ability to influence decisions	1	2	3	4	5
5. have ground rules that we adhere to	1	2	3	4	5

ATMOSPHERE (CONT.)

It is great to be on the team because we

6. trust each other	1	2	3	4	5
7. can speak our minds without fear	1	2	3	4	5
8. are treated like adults	1	2	3	4	5

LEADERSHIP

Our leader

1. is interested in what we have to say	1	2	3	4	5
2. consults us before making any changes affecting our work	1	2	3	4	5
3. looks for opportunities to delegate interesting work to us	1	2	3	4	5
4. encourages teamwork	1	2	3	4	5
5. acts as a coach (devotes enough time training us in key skills)	1	2	3	4	5
6. is concerned about our development	1	2	3	4	5
7. shares important information readily	1	2	3	4	5
8. is a person I respect	1	2	3	4	5

Measuring Team Performance

*I*f you don't measure something, you won't be able to manage it. The most effective way of measuring your team's performance is to involve your associates and customers in the process. A system called Performance Indexing has given organizations in every type of industry a boost since it

- ✓ involves the people who will take responsibility for performance improvement,
- ✓ gets the buy-in of the people who provide the product or service,
- ✓ focuses on the customer,
- ✓ measures a variety of indicators simultaneously,
- ✓ focuses on improvement.

The process of setting up a team score card requires the following 13 steps:

Step 1: Define the system.

Research is the first step. Work with your associates to answer the following questions:

- ✓ Who are our customers, internal and external?
- ✓ What are their needs?
- ✓ How are these needs being measured?
- ✓ How should they be measured?
- ✓ What products or services (outputs) are we currently supplying?
- ✓ What resources (inputs) are we using to meet our customers' needs? A description of the primary resources (people, materials, methods, equipment and capital) should be documented?

Step 2: Document your mission.

- Your team should document its mission. The mission will suggest what you should be measuring (see Mission Statements, page 219).
- A simple formula for writing up a mission is to answer these six questions:
  - ✓ Who are we?
  - ✓ What do we do?
  - ✓ How do we provide the product or service?
  - ✓ Who do we serve?
  - ✓ Where are our customers?
  - ✓ Why do we exist?
- Once these questions are answered, put them into one sentence and modify the wording until the message is clear and simple.

Step 3: Identify key performance indicators.

- Your work group needs to identify key indices in the most important categories of performance. These categories typically relate to
  - ✓ quality
  - ✓ cost effectiveness (profitability)
  - ✓ timeliness (service)
  - ✓ health and safety
- Your associates should reach consensus on what these indices are. Their input and agreement will build commitment that focuses on these key issues.
- Where possible, pick indicators that
  - ✓ are easy to collect
  - ✓ are already being collected
  - ✓ are accurate
  - ✓ you have control over

Step 4: Determine existing performance levels.

- Average the performance of the previous three months or another period.

- As you gather data, you will see how suitable your index is. If it becomes extremely costly to collect information for an indicator, then the indication's value should be questioned.
- Current performance levels should be entered on the table. Enter information in the boxes corresponding to the score of three. This will provide more room for improvement than for decline on the 0 to 10 scale (Figure 1).

Figure 1: Index Showing Existing Performance Levels

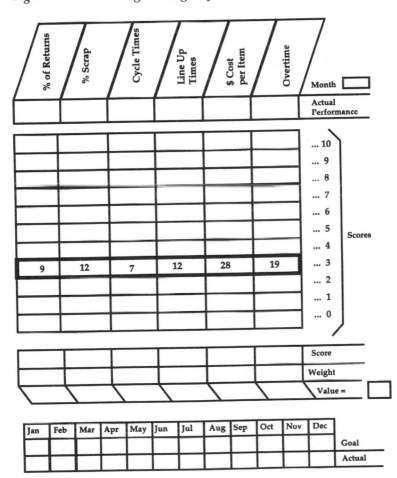

Step 5: Establish goals.

Next, the team should set goals. The goals should be SMART:

- ✓ **S**pecific;
- ✓ **M**easurable
- ✓ **A**greed-upon
- ✓ **R**ealistic;
- ✓ **T**ime-based

The goals should then be entered in the table at the level corresponding to the score of 10 (Figure 2).

Figure 2: Index Showing Goals

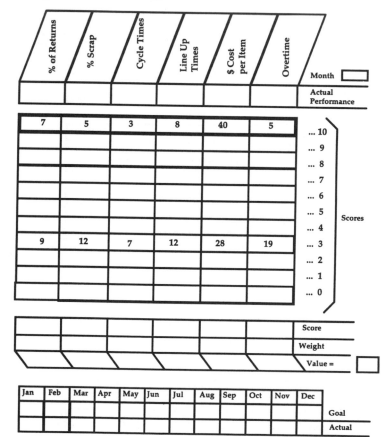

Step 6: Establish mini-goals.

The team will not improve from a score of 3 to 10 overnight. It may take a year. Therefore, it is important that the group be able to track its progress towards the final goal by setting mini-goals.

These mini-goals are entered in the table at the levels corresponding to the scores of 4, 5, 6, 7, 8 and 9 (Figure 3).

Figure 3: Setting Mini-goals

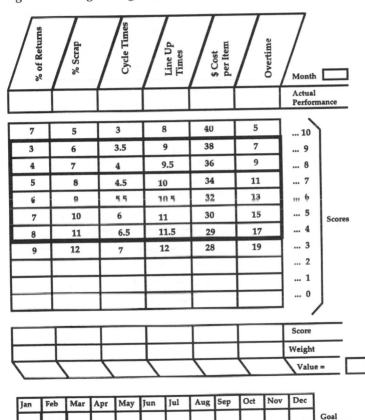

% of Returns	% Scrap	Cycle Times	Line Up Times	$ Cost per Item	Overtime	Month
						Actual Performance

% of Returns	% Scrap	Cycle Times	Line Up Times	$ Cost per Item	Overtime	Scores
7	5	3	8	40	5	... 10
3	6	3.5	9	38	7	... 9
4	7	4	9.5	36	9	... 8
5	8	4.5	10	34	11	... 7
6	9	5.5	10.5	32	13	... 6
7	10	6	11	30	15	... 5
8	11	6.5	11.5	29	17	... 4
9	12	7	12	28	19	... 3
						... 2
						... 1
						... 0

						Score
						Weight
						Value =

Jan	Feb	Mar	Apr	May	Jun	Jul	Aug	Sep	Oct	Nov	Dec	
												Goal
												Actual

Step 7: Establish the lower performance levels.

If performance declines, the team should record the declines in the table at levels 2, 1 and 0, with 0 being the worst possible level of performance (Figure 4).

Figure 4: Establishing Lower Performance Levels

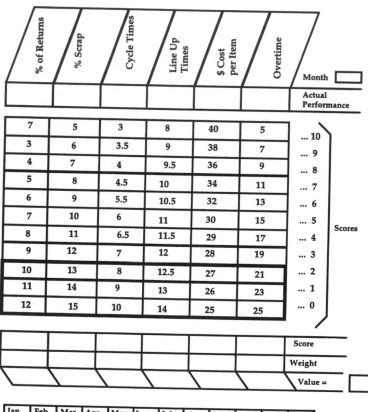

% of Returns	% Scrap	Cycle Times	Line Up Times	$ Cost per Item	Overtime	Month
						Actual Performance
7	5	3	8	40	5	... 10
3	6	3.5	9	38	7	... 9
4	7	4	9.5	36	9	... 8
5	8	4.5	10	34	11	... 7
6	9	5.5	10.5	32	13	... 6
7	10	6	11	30	15	... 5
8	11	6.5	11.5	29	17	... 4
9	12	7	12	28	19	... 3
10	13	8	12.5	27	21	... 2
11	14	9	13	26	23	... 1
12	15	10	14	25	25	... 0

Scores

						Score
						Weight
						Value =

Jan	Feb	Mar	Apr	May	Jun	Jul	Aug	Sep	Oct	Nov	Dec	
												Goal
												Actual

Step 8: Assign weights.

The team must decide the relative importance of each of the chosen indicators. Their decision should be recorded in the Weight section of the table. These weights should add up to 100%. This weighting, combined with the score, will allow the team to calculate its overall performance level each period (Figure 5).

Figure 5: Weighting

% of Returns	% Scrap	Cycle Times	Line Up Times	$ Cost per Item	Overtime	Month
						Actual Performance

% of Returns	% Scrap	Cycle Times	Line Up Times	$ Cost per Item	Overtime	Scores
7	5	3	8	40	5	... 10
3	6	3.5	9	38	7	... 9
4	7	4	9.5	36	9	... 8
5	8	4.5	10	34	11	... 7
6	9	5.5	10.5	32	13	6
7	10	6	11	30	15	... 5
8	11	6.5	11.5	29	17	... 4
9	12	7	12	28	19	... 3
10	13	8	12.5	27	21	... 2
11	14	9	13	26	23	... 1
12	15	10	14	25	25	... 0

						Score
15	20	10	10	30	15	Weight
						Value =

Jan	Feb	Mar	Apr	May	Jun	Jul	Aug	Sep	Oct	Nov	Dec	
												Goal
												Actual

Step 9: Allow development period.

The team will need some time — up to three months — to

- ✓ confirm current performance levels
- ✓ establish that the indices chosen are easy to collect data on
- ✓ devise the simplest way to collect accurate data
- ✓ develop an appropriate weighting system
- ✓ develop a plan of responsibility for the maintenance of the system and data collection and
- ✓ plan for improvement

Step 10: Plan for improvement.

- The team should divide itself into mini-teams that will be responsible for
  - ✓ collecting data on one index
  - ✓ collecting ideas for improvement
  - ✓ presenting ideas to the whole team
- Operating units should consider the following guidelines:
  - ✓ Focus on problems that members have control over.
  - ✓ Avoid working on problems where other people can provide support or knowledge. Ask for their help. Bring them into team meetings.
  - ✓ Break problems down into parts. Tackle them one at a time.
  - ✓ Prioritize plans. Your team has only limited resources and therefore must do whatever will give the biggest "bang for the bucks."
  - ✓ Work as a team. Involving your team will build commitment and produce better solutions.

Step 11: Tabulate scores and calculate the index at the end of each period.

At the conclusion of each weekly or monthly period the team should gather data and plot the results on your overall chart. The steps to follow are:

- ✓ Calculate the actual measure for each productivity indicator and enter it onto the performance line of the table.
- ✓ Circle the actual performance of each indicator on the scale. If a mini-goal is not achieved, the lower performance level should be circled. Any performance level lower than a score of 0 gets 0 for the period.
- ✓ Score the corresponding performance (0 to 10) and enter it on the score line of the table.
- ✓ Multiply the weighting factors by the score to get a weighted value. Enter the totals into the value line of the table.
- ✓ Add the weighted values together. The sum should equal the performance index for that monitoring period (see Figure 6). Over time, the movement of the index provides you with an excellent record of your change in performance.

Figure 6: Calculation of Performance Index

% of Returns	% Scrap	Cycle Times	Line Up Times	$ Cost per Item	Overtime	Month
						Actual Performance
7	5	3	8	40	5	... 10
3	6	3.5	9	38	7	... 9
4	7	4	9.5	36	9	... 8
5	8	4.5	10	34	11	... 7
6	9	5.5	10.5	(32)	13	... 6
7	10	6	(11.0)	30	(15)	... 5
(8)	11	6.5	11.5	29	17	... 4
9	(12)	7	12	28	19	... 3
10	13	(8)	12.5	27	21	... 2
11	14	9	13	26	23	... 1
12	15	10	14	25	25	... 0

Scores

4	3	2	5	6	5	Score
15	20	10	10	30	15	Weight
60	60	20	50	180	75	Value =

Jan	Feb	Mar	Apr	May	Jun	Jul	Aug	Sep	Oct	Nov	Dec	
												Goal
												Actual

Step 12: Plot the results.

The performance should be plotted on a graph against a target curve that should start at 300 and end at 1,000. A three-month moving average may be used and plotted to accommodate variations (see Figure 7).

Figure 7: Example of an Actual and Target Composite Index Plotted Monthly

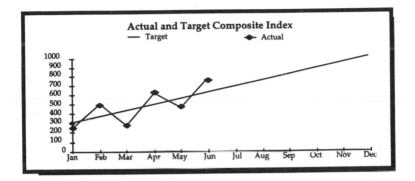

Step 13: Manage for improved performance.

- Meet regularly to review performance. At these meetings celebrate overall improvement as well as gains of individual indicators. If performance declines,
  - ✓ analyze the causes
  - ✓ find solutions
  - ✓ plan for improvement
  - ✓ take action

Commitment

We fail or succeed together. If we fail, no one is a winner.

BRENDA LAVIGNE, HUMAN RESOURCE MANAGER,
CUSTOM LEATHER CANADA

A project, team or department will stand or fall on whether its members are committed to its success. Your challenge as manager is to get that commitment, not from just one person but from the whole team or, quite often, from the whole department. This is how you do it:

- **Be prepared.** Have specific expectations worked out for each stage of the project. If you don't know what you want your team members to commit to, they won't perform.
- **Be clear.** You have a series of convincing arguments and facts that you used to put this project together — now use them on your team.
- **Be persuasive about the "boring stuff."** Budgets and deadlines on their own will not fire anyone's imagination, but tying them into the general vision of the project will make them compelling and will get your staff to buy in to bringing the project in on time and under budget.
- **Be open.** Encourage your team to make reasonable concerns known, to bring them out into the open where they can be addressed.
- **Be flexible.** If someone brings up a good point that you unaccountably missed, thank him or her, incorporate it and put your

own spin on it. This will give your colleague a sense of ownership in the project.

- **Be methodical.** Break down the project into sections, and have sets of goals, expectations and deadlines for each section. Discuss and approve every step.
- **Be perceptive.** If the room has suddenly started to clam up, you've either lost your team or something wasn't clear. Use humour to lighten the atmosphere and find out where the problem is. If you establish the right atmosphere, people will feel freer to voice their objections and suggestions, making buy-in stronger when these are addressed and resolved.
- **Be concise.** Get the message across quickly. Make it as easy to understand as possible without cluttering it up with unrelated or irrelevant information.
- **Follow up.** Type out the minutes of the meeting, append the expectations and working charts, get individual commitment to specific tasks and circulate the result. Post one copy on the team bulletin board so that all team members can refer to it.

Team Problem Solving

*You may be disappointed if you fail, but you
are doomed if you don't try.*

BEVERLEY SILLS, FORMER OPERA DIVA

*E*very person solves problems in his or her own particular way.
Therefore, while team problem solving can be very positive,
producing novel and innovative solutions with a lot of buy-in, it can
also be a problem if you're the one who has to co-ordinate everybody's decision-making styles. Here's how to get the benefits of team
decision-making without the disadvantages.

Identify the problem.
Channels of information include
- ✓ customer feedback
- ✓ attitude surveys
- ✓ personal observation
- ✓ deviation from quality and production goals

Assemble the team.
- Choose team members who are affected by the problem, have a
  stake in implementing any solution, have a creative bent for problem solving as demonstrated in the past and/or have the time
  available to work towards the best solution.
- Set ground rules for team meetings. These could include having
  a rotating chair who will ensure that no one talks over or interrupts anyone else and that everyone gets a chance to contribute,
  a simple resolution to start meetings on time and so on. Make

sure these rules are accepted by the team, written down and posted on the wall.

- Set operational guidelines: how often you will meet, where and when. How will team members communicate about team business between meetings? What, if any, deadlines exist? What roles are necessary to the problem-solving process and who will fill them? Get agreement to the answers to all of these questions and write the resolutions down.

Define the problem.

Ask Who, What, When, Where, Why and How (5 Ws and the H) to define the problem specifically. For example, if the problem is "an atmosphere of antagonism," try to narrow it down to "an atmosphere of antagonism between the marketing team and production team involved in Project X."

Find the cause.

- Establish the root cause of the problem. This can be done by
  - ✓ seeking the opinions of the people who are familiar with the issues and/or
  - ✓ analyzing any relevant data that points to key issues
- Again, use the 5 Ws and the H to ensure that the causes are clearly established.

Define the solution.

- Brainstorm and use a round robin to generate as many ideas as possible (see Creative Problem Solving). Once ideas are generated, start a round of piggybacking to build on the best ideas.
- Craft the most likely (cost-effective, time-effective and personnel-effective) solution(s) into an action plan, with specifically defined roles for each team member. Make sure the plan includes a concrete way to measure the success (or failure) of the plan, and specifically defined objectives (such as dates, times, quantities).

Implement the plan.

Evaluate and monitor the outcome.

- Use the specific indicators embedded in the action plan to measure the success of the solution at the next team meeting (the meetings should continue until the problem is seen to have been resolved).
- Assess the benefits and costs of the solution to the area of the company affected by the problem and its solution.
- Evaluate the efficacy of your solution.
- Document your solution and its benefits and post this on the department notice board as a template for other problem-solving teams to follow.
- Recognize the team by celebrating
    - ✓ the resolution of the problem and
    - ✓ the benefits that will accrue to the organization

Creative Problem Solving

Why not go out on a limb? Isn't that where the fruit is?

READER'S DIGEST

*M*ost people have had creativity drummed out of them by the time they've left the education system. However, the best solutions to difficult problems are the creative ones. Here's how to apply creativity to your problem solving:

Use people power.

- Every person who works on the solution to the problem will have a stake in implementing the solution. Include all those affected by the problem.
- Creativity is stimulated in a group environment, so deliberately select people with different skill sets, and those from different backgrounds, to offer the widest possible variety of viewpoints.
- Include at least one colleague who is thought to be a maverick, to act as a catalyst.

Get together.

- Choose an unusual and informal location for the meeting, to loosen up your team members and make them comfortable.
- Have an ice-breaker at the beginning of the meeting to get people talking — this could be anything from a short video to a plate of finger food.
- Make sure there is a flipchart in the room to record all the ideas generated, and appoint a recorder to write them down.

Brainstorm.

- The quantity of ideas is more important than the quality. Don't discuss or criticize the ideas right away, as this only reduces the time available for brainstorming.
- Conduct a round robin: go around the table in sequence and ask each person to propose an idea. The key here is speed — to get out as many ideas as possible. People who are out of ideas may pass.
- Piggyback ideas. This involves revisiting all the ideas on the flipchart and using them as inspiration for new ones, or variations on a theme. This is a good strategy when the group's ideas appear to have dried up.
- Incubate ideas after a creative session is over. Give everybody time to mull over the ideas proposed. This is a good strategy when it appears that the meeting has lost momentum — you simply schedule another session and send people home to think about the ideas put forth so far.

Evaluate.

When your team has come up with enough creative, workable ideas, you should evaluate them based on

- ✓ novelty
- ✓ cost
- ✓ benefit
- ✓ time to implement
- ✓ difficulty

Meetings

[Football] combines the two worst things about American life. It is violence, punctuated by a committee meeting.

GEORGE WILL, COLUMNIST AND BROADCASTER, OBSERVING YET ANOTHER HUDDLE AT A FOOTBALL GAME

Bad meetings are the bane of every manager's existence and the butt of every corporate joke. Still, for a team or a project to run smoothly, participants have to meet to pool ideas, compare notes and move forward. Here are some basic steps to help you run an outstanding meeting:

- Must you meet? Is there another way to share information? Keep in mind that time spent in meetings is time spent away from working on the project. If there is a more efficient way to exchange ideas and data, use it.
- Keep it simple. Invite only key players. Focus on a few items only.
- Prepare. Create a time-based agenda beforehand (see Setting an Agenda, page 112). Send the agenda and other necessary documents to the participants beforehand to allow them to prepare. And book the meeting room in advance.
- Start the meeting right:
  - ✓ Establish ground rules in advance and get buy-in on them.
  - ✓ Confirm the objective, time and process (method to deal with each agenda item).
  - ✓ Get organized. Involve team members in different roles. Assign someone to keep minutes, another to keep time, a

third to record key ideas on the flipchart and a fourth to ensure the ground rules are observed.

- Work through the agenda item by item, keeping to the schedule but ensuring each item is dealt with before moving on. Stay on track, and encourage others to do so. If some necessary materials were not passed out beforehand, distribute them as the relevant item comes up, so as not to distract the participants.
- Focus on the process. Allow participants to contribute to the content.
- Facilitate the process by asking questions, gettng agreement and summarizing as need be. Examples of questions to ask include
  - ✓ "What's next on the agenda?"
  - ✓ "How does everyone feel about this?"
  - ✓ "Are there any other opinions about this?"
  - ✓ "How much time do we have left?"
  - ✓ "How will we deal with [this issue]?"
  - ✓ "Should we take a vote?"
  - ✓ "Can everyone live with that?"
- Involve everybody. Don't let one or two people (including yourself) dominate the discussion. And, where possible, reach decisions by consensus. Make sure no one interrupts, talks over or intimidates anyone else. If necessary, assign a formal chairperson.
- Summarize and wrap up. Summarize each action point on the agenda and ensure that each has a plan of action, with a specific deadline (ASAP is not specific) and a person assigned to carry it out. Recap the action plan and ensure everyone is clear about what has been agreed upon.
- Send the minutes to participants and post them on the department bulletin board. Highlight each participant's commitment on his or her copy of the minutes.

MEETING CHECKLIST

To ensure good meetings, have one person keep a score sheet and provide you with feedback during the last five minutes of the meetings.

	Yes	No
• Before the meeting did you		
✓ inform the right people of the time and place?	❏	❏
✓ prepare your flipcharts or overheads?	❏	❏
✓ check equipment?	❏	❏
• At the start of the meeting did you		
✓ agree to an objective with the participants?	❏	❏
✓ agree how the meeting would be run? (process)	❏	❏
✓ agree on a time limit?	❏	❏
✓ have others keep time and write on the chart?	❏	❏
• During the meeting did you		
✓ ensure the agenda was visible?	❏	❏
✓ follow the agenda?	❏	❏
✓ keep on track?	❏	❏
✓ keep everyone involved?	❏	❏
✓ get agreements when necessary?	❏	❏
✓ listen carefully?	❏	❏
✓ record all key ideas?	❏	❏
• At the end of the meeting did you		
✓ summarize?	❏	❏
✓ set an action plan?	❏	❏

Things we want to do better at the next meeting:

1. _____

2. _____

3. _____

Setting an Agenda

*A*n agenda is a roadmap that will get you from A to B in the shortest possible time. Having a meeting without a plan is a formula for disaster. Here are some tips on how to develop your next agenda.

- Record meeting goals on paper. Be clear about what you want to achieve.
- Write out the steps or activities necessary to attain your goals.
- Analyze each step to identify whether it involves
  - ✓ presentation of information
  - ✓ feedback from participants
  - ✓ problem solving
  - ✓ decision making
  - ✓ planning
- Identify a process (method) to achieve results for each activity. Record the method in a separate column (see sample agenda below).
- Estimate how long each item on the agenda will take. This should be a lot easier now that you have a method or process.
- Include as the first item getting agreements on objectives, process, time and method by which you will make decisions.
- Next allow for a minute or two to get organized. You will want to appoint (or get volunteers as) a timekeeper, a secretary and a recorder for the flipchart. While this is typically done at the meeting, it can be done beforehand to save time.
- Record on your agenda the attendees, the starting and finishing times and the location.

- Allow time at the end for
  - ✓ developing action plans for decisions taken
  - ✓ summarizing the meeting
  - ✓ evaluating the meeting
- Circulate your agenda well in advance so that people can plan to attend and prepare their ideas.

SAMPLE AGENDA

Attendees:
Objectives: To reveiw a report and take action on key issues.
Date: September 16
Location: Board Room
Starting: 10 a.m.   **Concluding** at 11:15 a.m.

What (Content)	How (Process)	Time (Minutes)
• Agreements on objectives, time, process and how decisions will be made	Consensus	2
• Get organized	Timekeeper, recorder, secretary	2
• Present report	Overheads or flipcharts	5
• Feedback	Round robin	10
• Identify solutions	Brainstorming	10
• Pick best solution	Consensus	10
• Plan to implement	Action Plan	15
• Outstanding issues	Round robin	4
• Summary of meeting	Secretary to review minutes	4

Keeping Meetings Short

A meeting should go on only for as long as it takes to reach its objectives. Typically, this takes much longer than it should. Here's how you can shorten your meeting time dramatically:

Before the Meeting

- Ask yourself if the meeting is really necessary. If not, find an alternative, more efficient way of achieving your objective.
- Be clear about the objective. If you are not clear about what you want to achieve, no one else will be and the meeting will drift aimlessly.
- Make sure that the people who need to be present to make decisions can attend. If they can't attend, reschedule the meeting.
- Inform people in advance of the objective and agenda (see Setting an Agenda, page 112). Ask them to come prepared to deal with agenda items.

At the Meeting

- Start your meetings on time. Don't wait for latecomers.
- At the start of your meeting, get agreement on the objectives and time.
- Allocate specific times to each item on the agenda. This will allow you to better manage the time if certain items exceed their expected time allocation.
- Ask for a volunteer to be timekeeper. Ask the timekeeper to let you know if you are falling behind on any particular item on the agenda.
- Avoid going off track. If an unrelated issue is threatening to derail the discussion, offer to deal with it privately later.

- Set aside a "Parking Lot" on your flipchart. Then if issues unrelated to your meeting are brought up, ask that they be recorded in the Parking Lot and addressed later. Typically, when an idea is recognized, the person bringing it up will let go of it.
- Avoid repetition by recording ideas on the flipchart.
- Run stand-up meetings on the shop floor or in the office to avoid wasting time getting to meeting rooms. Also, people will want to sit after standing for more than 15 minutes, so they will be less likely to drag out discussions.
- Hold your meetings at the end of the day, scheduling them to finish at the official end of business. People will be motivated to finish on time.

Video-conferencing

While many companies now rely on video-conferencing over the Internet, it is unreliable unless

- All participants have top-notch, fast computers capable of running at a minimum of 500 MHz.
- You have access to wide bandwidth, such as that provided by your cable company. The ability to achieve television-like quality video requires access to a broad bandwidth of at least 300 kilobits per second (Kbps), or about six times the speed of the fastest currently available modems.
- You have access to third-party providers of video-conferencing. These specialists are able to offer high quality pictures with collaborative features such as file exchange, project management, "white boards" for brainstorming, chat rooms for break-out discussions, application sharing and slide shows.

Meeting in person is still best so you can gauge the enthusiasm for ideas from your observations of body language.

Problem Behaviour in Meetings

*M*eetings can often bring out undesirable or hindering behaviour in those who attend them. Here are some of the types of behaviour you'll face, along with tips on how to manage them effectively.

"Sidetrackers"

Formulate a firm agenda and stick to it.

- Make sure the agenda and ancillary materials are posted in a prominent place well in advance of the meeting.
- When setting the ground rules for the meeting, get a commitment that all will stick to the time allotted to each agenda item — if necessary, appoint a timekeeper.
- Allot a space on the flipchart for "related matters" to record side issues and agree to deal with the issues later, perhaps in another meeting.
- If someone goes off on a tangent, ask how his or her intervention is related to the item under discussion (sometimes it is — be prepared to allow for that).
- Use a pause in the person's commentary to say "Thank you, but I think we've veered off topic. Can we agree to get back to the agenda?"

"Wallflowers"

Encourage participation.

- Make sure that quiet people have all the advance documentation. This will enable them to be better prepared, and will increase their ability and willingness to contribute.

- Seat them next to you, make eye contact and, when you raise questions, call on them by name.
- Formulate your questions so that they require a simple "yes" or "no" response (these questions are much easier to answer than open-ended questions) and thank them for their contribution if they expand upon their answers.
- Canvass their opinions outside the meeting and raise their ideas yourself, giving them the credit. Appoint shy people to an inherently participatory position (flipchart recorder, round-robin moderator) and praise their efforts at the end of the meeting.
- Be aware that cultural and gender-based norms will keep some colleagues from speaking up — familiarize yourself with those obstacles and compensate for them as suggested above.

"Dominators"

Reverse the techniques you used to get shy people to talk.

- Place the person next to you but minimize eye contact. Look at everyone but the dominator when posing a question, and continually emphasize your desire to get everybody's opinion.
- When the dominator pauses to take a breath, interject with, "Thank you, what other opinions are there?" and call on the wallflower.
- If necessary, confer with the dominator outside the meeting and, while thanking him for his input, point out that everyone must be involved for a meeting to be successful. Ask for his help in bringing this about.

"Aggressors"

Remain calm.

- If the issue the aggressor has raised is legitimate, albeit off topic, allow her to vent and then, when you have established that she is finished, move on. If she becomes hostile, point out that this is not the meeting at which her item should be discussed — enter it in the "related matters" section of the flipchart and ensure her that it will be dealt with.

- If the aggressor persists in making exaggerated claims and foisting a political agenda onto the meeting, canvass his colleagues in the meeting to determine whether this opinion is isolated. If you determine that it is, state firmly, "Well, it looks as if no one else agrees with you, so why don't we agree to discuss this later," and move on to the next agenda item.
- Keep in mind that sometimes aggression in a meeting is symptomatic of difficulties only peripherally related to the meeting topic — confer with the aggressor outside the meeting, sharing your frustrations and concerns in a calm manner, and determine what the difficulty is. Ask for her help in ensuring that the next meeting runs smoothly and without hostility.

Attending Other People's Meetings

*A*s in all things, managers attending other people's meetings should extend the same courtesy they would expect at theirs. Here's how to be that key person you always want at your meetings.

Prepare, prepare, prepare.

- Read the agenda, if there is one — if there isn't, suggest that one be drawn up (see Setting an Agenda, page 112).
- Be aware of the timing of the meeting, and make arrangements to be free for at least the part for which you are required.
- Get all the key documents before the meeting and read them through at least once. If you have questions, note them in point form.

Participate.

- Start by getting to the meeting on time, and choose a seat that will allow you to make eye contact with the chairperson.
- Volunteer to take minutes, operate the flipchart or fill another useful role — if a manager offers to take on these tasks, it will give the participants a sense of the importance of the meeting.
- Listen to everyone's point of view without interrupting, and offer your comments and questions in a businesslike, objective manner. To avoid confusion, ask that unclear points be summarized or paraphrased.

Expedite.

- Do your part to see that the agenda and schedule are followed, by offering to be timekeeper. Look at your watch when discussions start to drag, steering the meeting back onto topic during tangential discussions by asking for the next agenda item, and, as a last resort, asking whether your presence is required for the remaining items on the agenda.

- Do not participate in sidebar discussions. Summarize issues to bring them to a close (see Keeping Meetings Short, page 114).

Recap.

- If the meeting content is not clear, offer to summarize the discussion and decisions.
- Request a copy of the minutes and the post-meeting memo, and emphasize the need for specific item deadlines.
- Make sure you know what your (and your team's) particular obligations are, and post them prominently on the team bulletin board.

PART IV

Leadership

Leadership

Do not go where the path may lead. Go instead
where there is no path and leave a trail.

RALPH WALDO EMERSON (1803–82)

The definition of leadership is changing as the business world changes, but one fact remains constant — to be a good manager, you must be a leader. Here's how to maximize your leadership skills:

Look to the future.

- Have a vision — for your company, for your team, for yourself. Articulate this vision and share it, winning others to it. Emphasize the vision at every opportunity.
- Teach others about new technologies and innovations in product and process, and let others teach you. Leaders bring all their colleagues into the future with them.
- Be a risk-taker and try new ideas. Those who fail to accept challenges stagnate and are passed by.
- Encourage others to innovate. Allow yourself to be influenced when a new idea is brought to you and seems sound.

Be human.

- Be willing to make mistakes and learn from them. Admit it when you make a mistake. Allow others to be human and make mistakes. But don't make the same mistake twice.
- Listen carefully to people, and respond to them. Don't interrupt.
- Treat every staff member as an individual, and with respect.
- Walk the talk — do as you tell others to do.
- Don't betray confidences.

- Involve people in decisions, especially those that will affect them.
- Stick to your principles.

Work smarter, not harder.

- Be flexible and adaptable, always learning and modifying based on new information.
- Be co-operative and encourage co-operation in your team.
- Be able to fill a number of roles — conciliator, facilitator, mentor, manager, evaluator.
- Acknowledge excellence in others and encourage it. Don't be threatened by it.
- Give credit where credit is due — to yourself and to others.
- Get the job done without procrastination and with a minimum of politics.

Develop your team.

- Recruit great people. Find people who are more capable than you.
- Develop those who are not naturally talented. Spend at least 60% of your time developing people so that they can take care of business for you.
- Encourage teamwork. Measure your progress and display the results. Celebrate successes.
- Get agreement on your values. Reward those who follow those values and let those who do not know of your dissatisfaction. Give feedback on individual and team performance regularly.

Decision Making

Nothing is more difficult, and therefore more precious, than to be able to decide.

NAPOLEON BONAPARTE (1769–1821)

*H*ow decisions are made has a lot to do with how effective the decisions turn out to be.

- Recognize that there are many ways to make decisions. Most commonly, decisions can be made by
  - ✓ one person or a few people (minority)
  - ✓ most people (majority) or
  - ✓ with everyone's support (consensus)
- Learn what decision-making methods are appropriate for each situation.
- Minority decisions can be made when
  - ✓ there is lack of time
  - ✓ there is an emergency
  - ✓ the issue relates to health and safety
  - ✓ the decision is strategic
  - ✓ one person is the acknowledged expert
- The majority opinion should be used to make decisions when
  - ✓ a decision is required quickly
  - ✓ there are too many people to negotiate a consensus
  - ✓ the issue is very divisive
- Decisions that affect your associates and require their commitment should be made by consensus.
- If you want your team to reach a consensus, let everyone know the place and time for the meeting in advance. With a few days'

notice all will have time to consider alternative ideas and arrive at the meeting with an informed choice.

- At your meeting, you can reach consensus quickly using the Nominal Group Technique. This process consists of eight critical steps:
  1. **Set a goal.** "We want to reach consensus on _____."
  2. **Agree on the process.** Ask participants if they will support the majority. Any other constraints should also be agreed to.
  3. **Generate ideas silently.** Participants record their ideas.
  4. **Collect ideas by round robin.** Each member gives an idea in turn. These ideas are recorded without discussion.
  5. **Clarify and lobby.** Key ideas are evaluated in greater detail. If you have a long list, vote to establish the top five. Next, spend time evaluating each idea by looking at pros and cons.
  6. **Take a vote.** Participants make their choices: for example, first choice gets 5 points, second choice gets 3 points, third choice gets 1 point. Alternatively, members can vote on all items they consider significant.
  7. **Tally the votes.** The leader counts the votes for each idea and identifies the top choice(s).
  8. **Check for consensus.** The leader checks to see if everyone either agrees with the majority or, at least, supports the most popular choice.

- If you cannot reach a consensus, your options are to
  ✓ tell people what your decision will be if no consensus is reached
  ✓ ask people to listen to one another and be accommodating
  ✓ review each position by canvassing each person, one at a time
- If rigidity persists, you should make the decision. In general, people will find this acceptable since they did have a chance to reach a consensus first.
- For more complex decisions use a table or tally sheet (see the example that follows).

ITEM	IMPORTANCE	COST	EASE OF IMPLEMENTATION	VALUE TO CUSTOMER	OTHER	TOTAL

Note: Score 1 to 5 for each item in each column; 1 = worst, 5 = best.

- Allow each person to evaluate each idea by ranking it in terms of the agreed-to criteria. Collect the sheets and create a master tally sheet.
- Use the tally sheet for Step 6 of the Nominal Group Technique. It is important that people agree in advance to support the majority, and that they confirm their support when the most popular choice is revealed.

Change Management

The future isn't what it used to be.

ANONYMOUS

S ome people thrive on change and some people would rather avoid it, but both can benefit from it and, given proper preparation, enjoy it. Change is an opportunity for success as well as for failure. Focus on the possibility of success, and encourage others to do so. Oysters don't like sand much, but they make beautiful pearls of it. Here's how to make change a positive experience for everyone involved (including you):

- Realize that change is inevitable, and plan for it. Assess in advance its impact on
  - ✓ you
  - ✓ your team
  - ✓ your division
  - ✓ your boss
- Find out what kind of change is coming. Is it an update in technology? A merger? A legal shift? How urgent is it, and who is driving it? What are their motivations? Answers to these questions will give a you a clearer picture of what's ahead and help you to help others prepare for it.
- Evaluate your people's ability to absorb the change. Their adaptability may be influenced by previous experiences, their length of service and your style of leadership.
- Whenever possible, give your associates advance notice of pending changes so that they have time to adjust. Rally your people to meet the challenge together.

- When you communicate change to those around you, describe it in the context of "the big picture." Show how the change will affect your corporate mission and goals.
- Explain how changes will affect each person. People are fearful of things that affect them directly: changing routines, losing jobs or being moved to new areas. Be available to answer questions and listen to concerns.
- Prepare people by giving them the tools to master changes in processes or technology. Provide them with seminars, hands-on experiences and trips to companies that have made similar changes.
- Show people how they can benefit from change. If the task requires more effort, skill or responsibility, provide rewards such as higher pay, more time off or specialized training.
- Listen to your people's ideas on how to make change as smooth as possible. Their involvement will increase their commitment.
- Ask for new ideas soon after a change has been made so that you reinforce the fact that change is constant.

Dealing with Failure

- Some of your plans for change will fail. Treat failure as a learning experience. Analyze what you did wrong so that you don't make the same mistake again.
- If you have failed, don't give up. Get up, dust yourself off and try again and again, until you succeed.
- Let others benefit from your mistakes. Inform your peers of problems you encountered so that they can avoid the same pitfalls.
- Let your associates know that it is permissible to fail. However, encourage them to take responsibility for fixing their mistakes and learning from them.
- Set a time frame for analyzing and evaluating the results of your change.

Evaluating Team Readiness for Change

Ask your people to complete the following survey anonymously. Collect the responses, analyze the data and modify your implementation to suit your circumstances.

This survey will help us introduce change in our work area with the least disruption. Please help me by completing the survey and returning it in the enclosed envelope.

Signed _____

Read the statements below and circle the responses that best reflect how you feel: 1 = strongly disagree; 2 = disagree; 3 = neither agree or disagree; 4 = agree; 5 = strongly agree.

- Change usually creates
  more problems than
  solutions.   1   2   3   4   5
- Before making changes,
  my boss asks my opinion.   1   2   3   4   5
- Change is needed here.   1   2   3   4   5
- I never hear about changes
  until they are made.   1   2   3   4   5
- When changes are made
  here, employees always
  seem to lose out.   1   2   3   4   5
- I don't look forward to
  changes.   1   2   3   4   5

Overcoming Resistance to Change

The science of today is the technology of tomorrow.

Edith Teller

*N*ever assume that people will be as excited about a new idea as you are. People usually see obstacles before benefits. As a leader, you need to nurture acceptance as quickly and as painlessly as possible. Here are some useful ideas:

- Demonstrate your own commitment in meaningful ways. For example, show that you are investing resources in the new concept.
- Evaluate how committed people are. If there is resistance, find out why. Hold a meeting. Ask for reasons without personalizing, attacking or being defensive.
- When aware of the reasons, remove the problem. If the problem is misperception, show things as they really are, giving examples or illustrations. If the concern is lack of skills, offer training.
- Offer support and encouragement during the transition. Indicate your willingness to accept some level of imperfection and mistakes throughout the transition. This will reduce people's fears of failure.
- Give as much information as possible. Focus on information that will be relevant to your people.
- Involve people in identifying ways to demonstrate their commitment. The greater their involvement, the greater their commitment.

- Negotiate goals that can be used to evaluate people's commitment. These should be specific, measurable and realistic. Set a meeting to evaluate progress.
- Recognize the phases that most people experience during change:
  ✓ denial
  ✓ anger
  ✓ acceptance
  ✓ action

Make people aware of these phases, indicating that these reactions are normal. Help your people deal with the transition.

Listening

The older I grow, the more I listen to people who don't say much.

GERMAINE G. GLIDDEN

Y ou cannot learn without listening, and you cannot lead without learning. Many business disasters have come to pass simply because no one was listening when a problem was brought to the table. On the positive side, listening will increase your influence, the confidence of your staff and the reserve of information with which you can make informed decisions. Here are the guidelines of good listening:

- **Pay attention.** Give the other person your full attention. Set aside your work and do not take phone calls while you are listening.
- **Meet in a quiet place.** Step away from any noise or distractions that may hinder your listening.
- **Focus on listening.** Listen to be influenced without developing a rebuttal partway through the process. Don't allow your mind to leap ahead to arguments or conclusions. Simply take in the message you are being given.
- **Don't interrupt.** Let the other person finish her thoughts and ideas. Only stop a monologue when the same point is being rehashed again and again. Then you may interrupt to indicate that you have heard and understood.
- **Let the person speak.** Even when the other person is stumbling to make a point, don't interrupt or correct him. Get in the habit of counting to five before you interject or respond.

- **Show your interest.** You can do this by nodding, saying "yes," or changing your facial expressions to reflect the message you are taking in.
- **Be there.** Maintain good eye contact. Don't stare, but give your full visual attention to the other person.
- **Keep track of your body language.** Your posture reflects your attitude. You can demonstrate an open, receptive attitude by
  - ✓ leaning forward
  - ✓ looking interested
  - ✓ facing the other person
  - ✓ smiling or showing your reactions with your facial expressions
- **Check your understanding.** You want to be sure you understand what is being said. One way to do this is to ask, "So what you are saying is _____. Is that right?" Allow the person to correct you if you have misunderstood.
- **Ask questions.** Questions show your interest and check your understanding, to help you get at the feelings behind the facts.
- **Keep an eye on non-verbal reactions** (see Reading Body Language, page 54). People display their feelings and opinions without uttering a word. The gestures, eye movements, posture and facial expressions of others can tell you more than their words.
- **Stay with the speaker.** Don't leap to conclusions. Refrain from filling in the gaps. Stop yourself from formulating responses ahead of time.
- **Don't rush ahead.** Don't finish the other person's sentences for her.
- **Show empathy.** Even if you disagree with what the other person is saying, he must have a reason for saying it. Try to understand that reason and his point of view.
- **Accept silence.** Learn to accept the brief, natural lulls in conversation. Silence encourages the other person to continue sharing.

Counselling

Don't fret if the temptation to give advice is overwhelming, because the tendency to ignore it is universal.

UNKNOWN

Sometimes employees' personal problems interfere with their job performance. If this occurs, a manager must step in to address the problem.

Preparation

- Collect the facts. Data will be more useful than opinions. Note how much performance has declined.
- Set clear objectives. Know what you want to achieve when the process is over.
- Make notes about what you intend to say. Rehearse your introduction to ensure a smooth start to the meeting.
- Schedule an appointment to meet. Set aside at least 30 minutes for the interview.
- Meet in a neutral office or meeting room. Privacy is essential.
- Organize the furniture to promote a problem-solving atmosphere. Sit next to the associate.
- Plan to take notes of agreements and action plans.

During the Interview

- Greet employees warmly, but don't try to soften them up with praise that is unrelated to the discussion. The faster you get down to dealing with the issue the better.
- Describe the problem. Give examples.

- Encourage your associate to help find the cause of the problem. Ask open-ended questions such as
  ✓ Do you have any idea why that happens?
  ✓ What do you think is the problem?
- Listen emphatically. Show your support and confidence in the associate's ability to solve the problem.
- If the person is reluctant to discuss the problem, ask if the problem concerns personal matters. If so, you have two options:
  1. If the person is comfortable discussing the matter with you and is confident in your ability to assist, take a problem-solving approach: encourage the employee to identify the problem, its primary cause and possible solutions. It's important to have the employee resolve the issue, to develop their problem-solving skills and buy-in to the solution. Arrange a follow-up meeting at which you can monitor progress and show your continued interest in the matter.
  2. If the person is not comfortable discussing personal matters, ask if professional help is an option. If acceptable, obtain counselling quickly. Follow up as needed to assure your support and continued interest.
- If your associate refuses to discuss the problem, and the problem is affecting performance, you will have to surmise the cause and identify your own solutions.
- When you establish the cause, ask what the associate will do about it. If there is more than one solution, make a list. Have the associate evaluate each solution.
- Don't take responsibility for solving the problem. Your associate must make the decisions. Ask for a commitment within a definite time period.
- Summarize your discussion to avoid future uncertainty.

After the Interview
- Follow up to ensure that agreed-upon actions have been taken. Show appreciation for positive change. If no change has

occurred, repeat the procedure, emphasizing consequences if improvement does not take place. Consequences might include

✓ a note in the file
✓ a time off without pay
✓ termination

Coaching

The final test of a leader is that he leaves behind in other men the conviction and the will to carry on.

WALTER LIPPMANN (1889–1974), AMERICAN JOURNALIST

Good coaches train their people to do the job right every time. While most coaching is done in technical areas of a job, you can also coach your people to improve their team and interpersonal skills.

- Meet daily with people — either collectively or one on one — to obtain agreement on what is expected of them.
- Measure each person's performance. Allow him or her to have input into the best indicator(s).
- Encourage people to be aware of their performance and take ownership of improvement.
- Use these methods to help your people reach their goals:
  ✓ **Coaching.** Demonstrate the skills you expect others to use.
  ✓ **Mentoring.** Help your associates find solutions through step-by-step self-discovery.
  ✓ **Training.** Increase your associates' skills with on-the-job training. Start by explaining what you want them to do, showing them how to do it, letting them try while you observe and giving them feedback on their performance.
  ✓ **Confronting.** Let your associates know when their behaviour fails to meet agreed-upon standards (see Giving Feedback, page 154).

- If associates fail to do the job right, redirect them. Show them again. Ask them to confirm their understanding of the task. Have them demonstrate their understanding by showing you how to do the task.
- If the task is large or appears difficult, break it into pieces. Learning one step at a time will build the trainee's self-confidence.
- If associates do not improve after a number of trials, determine whether the cause is attitudinal or a lack of aptitude. If it is the latter, move them to jobs that better suit their skill sets. If it is attitudinal, determine the cause (see Counselling, page 135) and the solution. If this does not work — and only a small minority will not respond — go through the disciplinary procedure and terminate the individual.
- Give people regular feedback. Wherever possible, measure their performance so that they know whether they are improving or getting worse.
- As people's skills improve, encourage them to discover new and better ways of doing things. Praise them for their new ideas.
- Allow people to improvise. Even if the new method does not fit your perception of the best method, encourage a spirit of enterprise.

Mentoring

*M*entoring is a process focused on the development of one person by another. Through regular contacts, the mentor guides and nurtures the protégé towards an agreed-upon goal. This process enables the protégé to make a greater contribution to the organization.

Mentoring is one of a number of options that an organization can use to further the development of its people. Unfortunately, mentoring programs work in only about 50% of organizations that embark on the process. But there are number of things that mentors can do to ensure that the relationship does not end in failure. As a mentor, consider these actions before beginning a partnership with a protégé:

Before Starting

- Establish whether your organization has a mentoring program. If it does, and it has been well designed, take advantage of the service, which will
  - ✓ match your talents with the needs of a protégé
  - ✓ provide you with the tools — forms, systems and training — to manage the process
  - ✓ provide you with ongoing advice as needed
- Take advantage of training programs that will focus on giving you the tools to
  - ✓ get the process started on the right foot
  - ✓ set goals with your protégé
  - ✓ help your protégé develop a training plan that is compatible with her learning needs and style
  - ✓ assist the protégé in identifying his own solutions to problems

✓ provide effective feedback to the protégé
✓ know when and how to bring the relationship to a happy conclusion
- Insist that your protégé also get suitable training before you begin. Such training will help her to
  ✓ become a full partner in the process
  ✓ set her own goals for the relationship
  ✓ understand her role and responsibilities
  ✓ give you feedback on your performance

Starting the Process

- After each of you has the skills to make the relationship work, set up your first meeting. The focuses of the meeting should be to
  ✓ get to know each other
  ✓ clarify the objectives for the relationship
  ✓ estimate how long the process is likely to take
  ✓ decide how often you will meet
  ✓ pick a place for ongoing meetings
  ✓ set up ground rules for the relationship (see "Typical Ground Rules for a Mentoring Relationship," page 142)

Maintaining the Relationship

- Maintain the effectiveness of your relationship by
  ✓ ensuring that each meeting has clear objectives
  ✓ following up on previously agreed-upon goals and action items
  ✓ dealing with items systematically, one at a time
  ✓ ensuring that each decision taken is recorded in an action plan, together with a date by which it will be completed
- Learn to influence your protégé:
  ✓ Avoid giving straight answers to his questions. Rather, ask him for his opinion. If you are unable to get an opinion from your protégé, provide him with some alternatives. Then ask him which one would be most acceptable and why. This will

help him develop his self-confidence and problem-solving abilities.

✓ Illustrate a solution through a story of your personal experience. Let her then figure our whether your solution might work for her.

✓ Allow him to teach you. Listen intently to his ideas. Mentors can learn, too.

- Bring the relationship to a graceful, successful conclusion. You will know that the time is drawing near when

  ✓ the meetings are getting shorter
  ✓ there is less and less to discuss
  ✓ the discussions are becoming less focused

- Celebrate the achievements of the relationship by

  ✓ informing human resources that you will not be meeting formally any longer
  ✓ inviting your protégé to give you formal feedback, evaluating what worked well for you
  ✓ having a meal together so that you can toast your mutual achievements
  ✓ writing a letter to the protégé recording your feelings about her and letting her know how you have benefited from the relationship

---

TYPICAL GROUND RULES FOR A MENTORING RELATIONSHIP

We both agree to

✓ maintain a focus for our discussions
✓ make our meetings a priority, and not cancel them unless absolutely necessary
✓ keep confidential anything discussed between us
✓ respect one another's ideas, even though we may not always agree with each other
✓ keep an open mind in discussing issues
✓ listen to and respect each other

Delegating

*The highest manifestation of life is this: that a
being governs its own actions. A thing which is
always subject to the direction of another is
somewhat of a dead thing.*

St. Thomas Aquinas (1225–74)

A s a leader, you will be judged as much by what happens when you
are present as by what happens when you are absent.

Good managers never put off till tomorrow what they can delegate today. A major cause of stress and poor time management is
an unwillingness, or inability, to delegate responsibility to people
who work for us. Delegating responsibility to others allows you to
concentrate on your duties as manager: planning, problem solving
and other pro-active matters. Failure to delegate forces you to spend
too much time on trivial issues and to neglect critical opportunities.
Here's what you can do to correct the situation:

In General

- Write down all your activities for one week. Categorize them as A
  and B activities. All or most A activities can be delegated, including
  ✓ routine work
  ✓ data collection
  ✓ attending meetings unrelated to adding value for internal or
    external clients
- You will be left with more enriching tasks, the B activities, that
  will use your conceptual and communication abilities, including
  ✓ strategic planning
  ✓ coaching

✓ goal setting
✓ problem solving
✓ communicating with customers
✓ carrying messages between those above and below you

- Accept that you cannot do everything, be everywhere and make all decisions. Believe that your people are capable of doing more of your mundane work without much difficulty.
- Identify people who could take some of the load off your shoulders. These people
  ✓ have an interest in the job
  ✓ have or will make the time to do the jobs you delegate
  ✓ have the skills to do the jobs
- If people have the time and inclination but not the skills, train them.

At a Delegation Meeting

- Explain the purpose.
- Describe the task you want done.
- Be specific about the goal.
- Stress how important it is that the task be done in a timely and accurate manner.
- Obtain agreement about the goal.
- Agree on a date by which the task will be completed.
- If the task is big, establish mini-goals with corresponding timelines.
- Discuss benefits that people might enjoy as a result of taking on the new job. These might include increased responsibility, learning opportunities, added exposure in the organization or promotion opportunities.
- Make sure that the person accepts the task and its scope. A handshake is an acceptable way of acknowledging acceptance.
- Assign responsibility and authority. Tell your associates how confident you are in their ability to do the job.

- Ask if the associate foresees any problems in carrying out the task. Help to resolve any problems.

After the Meeting

- Monitor people as needed to ensure directions are clearly understood.
- Monitor performance closely at first and then less frequently. If associates are performing well, let them know. If not, give them appropriate feedback, focusing on the behaviour, not the person.
- Show confidence in people by giving them some freedom to do the task their way.
- Ensure that people who work with you and your associate know that you have delegated the task and that you have given the associate the authority to do the job.

Motivating

> *There are no people who aren't capable of
> doing more than they think they can do.*
>
> HENRY FORD (1863–1947),
> AMERICAN AUTOMOBILE MANUFACTURER

*M*otivation is the skill of getting great performance from your average associate. But you cannot motivate your people: they need to motivate themselves. What you can do is create the climate in which motivation will blossom.

- Expect the most from your people. Your behaviour will reflect your confidence. You will not supervise too closely. You will trust them. You will delegate responsibility.
- Treat associates like adults. Adults are respected and listened to. Adults are allowed to make decisions without constant evaluation and criticism. Adults are trusted with important information.
- Treat your associates as you would your customers. Regularly, ask them for feedback on how you are doing. Listen to their comments and take action to improve yourself.
- Recognize people for a job well done. People feel good when they are made to feel special. Their confidence grows. They also become more willing to take on increasingly tough tasks.
- Be clear about your expectations. Be specific.
- Set goals with, not for, people. Involve them in determining SMART goals:
  - ✓ **S**pecific
  - ✓ **M**easurable
  - ✓ **A**greed-upon

✓ **R**ealistic

✓ **T**ime-based

Involvement leads to commitment. Commitment leads to achievement. Achievement allows you to recognize and reward people.

- Give your associates regular feedback (see Giving Feedback, page 154). Don't wait till the annual performance appraisal.
- Trust your people. Allow them to make decisions without being closely monitored. Also, let them make mistakes and learn from these mistakes by fixing them.
- Don't hover around people. It will make them nervous and undermine their confidence.
- Treat your people as individuals, not as statistics. Show an interest in them. Find out about outside activities, interests and families. Find something that you have in common with them and use it to establish rapport.
- Meet with associates regularly to review
  - ✓ how you are doing as a coach
  - ✓ what help they need to do their jobs better
  - ✓ what changes would make their jobs better or easier
  - ✓ what they like best, and least
  - ✓ what they do best, and worst
  - ✓ what their priorities in the jobs are
- Allow people to make the decisions in their own work area, to increase their confidence and give them a sense of ownership.
- Train people who want more responsibility. They will be able to do a greater variety of tasks and handle more complex duties.
- Keep people informed. Share important information. Take them into your confidence. Make them feel important.
- Never betray the confidence of your associates. Keep private matters to yourself.
- Identify people's strengths. Find out what special achievements they have made outside work. Put these skills to work for you.
- Don't allow failure to destroy the self-confidence of your people.

Encourage them to try again, emphasizing out your confidence in them.

- Challenge people with an increasing number of tasks and decisions. Allow them time and space to grow. The more they do, the quicker they can absorb some of your less challenging tasks, giving you more time to tackle those that require your best skills.
- Provide people with opportunities to participate fully as team members. For example, rotate meeting facilitators.
- Meet daily with them. Let them know your priorities. If you need to change priorities, explain why.
- Respect people's time. Don't ask them to do things that others should be doing, unless it is an emergency. Don't continuously interrupt them unless absolutely necessary. Let them complete each task.
- Introduce your assistant to key associates and customers. All parties will be more comfortable resolving issues in your absence.
- Inform your people where you are, how you can be reached, and when you will be returning. Pressure to track you down during a crisis is an unnecessary burden.
- Don't treat your people as scapegoats when things go wrong, especially if you are the cause of the problem. You will destroy their trust in you and undermine your working relationship.
- Provide people with the encouragement, time and money needed to upgrade their skills. This investment in their training demonstrates your long-term commitment to them.

Encouraging Creativity

> *The reasonable man adapts himself to the world. The unreasonable man persists in trying to adapt the world to himself. Therefore, all progress depends on the unreasonable man.*
>
> GEORGE BERNARD SHAW (1856–1950)

*A*s a manager, you must ensure that your associates are given the opportunity to contribute new, innovative solutions. The following strategies will help you.

- Look for creative people. They
  - ✓ may be unconventional (in their approach, dress, etc.)
  - ✓ often appear to be troublemakers
  - ✓ are persistent
  - ✓ are willing to take risks
  - ✓ have vivid imaginations
- Encourage your creative people to take risks by rewarding efforts and process, not only results. Doing so sends a clear message that the action is as important as the outcome.
- Accept small improvements rather than expect major ones; base hits are important since they prepare people to strive for home runs later on.
- Set up a budget for experimentation to show your interest in new initiatives.
- Allow mistakes. It's impossible to make significant improvements without errors. Don't look at failure as the end of the road. Rather, consider it a stepping stone. Involve your people in finding out what went wrong and how obstacles can be overcome.

- Support persistence. Not all innovations come from flashes of imagination. Sometimes real innovations come from hours, days and even years of trial and error.
- Be open and responsive to new ideas. Listen to be influenced rather than to concentrate on developing a rebuttal.
- If you find it difficult to assess the merits of a new idea, find someone who can and who might advocate on behalf of the idea.
- Maintain a relaxed atmosphere. Having fun creates a playful environment that encourages creative actions.
- Encourage foolish or impractical ideas, particularly those that don't have an immediately negative influence on your business. These ideas can often be built on and can lead to new innovations.
- Challenge people to come up with new ideas daily.
- Leave a flipchart in the work area. Encourage people to record ideas as they occur. Share and evaluate their ideas with your people at your next meeting.
- Go outside your business to look for new ideas that could work in your area. While you may get ideas from similar work areas within your organization, you will find more innovative solutions in other organizations and industries.
- Challenge yourself and your workers to think of more reasons why a new idea would work, rather than reasons why it would not.
- Increase the value of your ideas by applying the SCAMPER process:
  - ✓ **S**ubstitute similar items to form new products (e.g., plastic for metal).
  - ✓ **C**ombine distinctly different items to produce a synergistic product or service (e.g., helium and engine to make a blimp).
  - ✓ **A**dapt, add to, or adjust similar items (e.g., add another blade to make a twin-blade shaving system).
  - ✓ **M**odify, magnify or minimize for other uses.
  - ✓ **P**ut pieces to other uses (e.g., a newspaper for packing).
  - ✓ **E**liminate unnecessary elements.
  - ✓ **R**everse or rearrange items.

Empowering

A candle loses nothing of its light by lighting another candle.

JAMES KELLER

You will get the most out of people if you treat them as partners and give them increasing power as their abilities improve.

- Accept the fact that you are fallible. Learn from others, particularly from someone who does the job regularly.
- Concern yourself with the process your people are using as well as the outcome.
- Allow people to discover their own ways to achieve goals.
- Encourage people to take responsibility for their decisions by giving them an opportunity to self-correct and learn from their mistakes.
- Establish clear boundaries. Be prepared to enlarge these boundaries as confidence and competence grow.
- Review your management systems regularly to ensure that they support rather than obstruct performance.
- Train your people continuously. This will increase their skills and confidence.
- Develop and nurture personal relationships based on respect, inclusion and trust. Treat others as you want to be treated.
- Be patient and do not become discouraged if people don't jump at the first opportunity to take on new challenges. They may be suspicious of your motives — with good reason.
- Walk your talk! Consistent support will help overcome people's suspicions, and they will jump at the opportunities you provide.

Providing Recognition

> *One of my bosses had a way of saying nice things about his workers that got back to them. True things but nice things. We appreciated it, and we couldn't keep from trying to do more things that he could tell others about. People will work hard to uphold a good reputation.*
>
> FRED SMITH, CEO, FEDERAL EXPRESS

*E*mployee attitude surveys reveal that people do not feel appreciated and are seldom told when they do a good job. These same people typically complain that they get instant feedback when they make a mistake. Here's how you can rectify the situation:

- Relate rewards to job performance rather than to factors such as seniority that have little or nothing to do with effort and skill.
- Set goals or standards with your people individually and in teams. These should be specific, measurable, reasonable, yet challenging.
- Recognize people immediately so that there is a clear link between performance and reward.
- Personalize the recognition. Treat each person individually but within similar boundaries. For example, don't reward one person with a pat on the back and another with a day off work for similar achievements.
- Vary the ways you recognize people so that the process does not become mundane. Some ways to show your appreciation are
  - ✓ an oral thank you
  - ✓ a written commendation
  - ✓ upbeat comments on Post-it Notes at person's workplace

- ✓ a gift
- ✓ time off
- ✓ a free meal
- ✓ thanks, oral or written, from a senior manager
- ✓ praise in front of peers
- ✓ praise at a management meeting
- ✓ praise in the newsletter
- ✓ a plaque
- ✓ an award at a banquet
- Periodically acknowledge people in front of their peers: it sends a clear message about the things that are important to you. Public recognition is appropriate for such things as an excellent
  - ✓ team effort
  - ✓ health and safety record
  - ✓ attendance record
- Reward people who have worked excessive overtime at the expense of their family life by sending
  - ✓ a letter of thanks to their families
  - ✓ flowers to their homes
  - ✓ a voucher for a family dinner
- Don't overdo recognition. Constant compliments to staff will turn the process into a mockery.

Giving Feedback

*T*he most important skill in a manager's repertoire is the ability to communicate effectively to associates what you think of their performance, be it positive or negative. Often, managers fail to deal with this issue altogether, thereby condoning poor performance and frustrating those who put in the extra effort to compensate for it. Positive and negative feedback are two sides of the same coin, and both must be delivered in a professional, forthright manner to ensure maximum effect.

Positive Reinforcement

When you catch someone exceeding your expectations, let her know of your appreciation and approval.

- Tell her soon.
- Be specific about what it is that you appreciate. Saying "thank you for completing your report two days early" is better than "You're doing a great job."
- Let her know how you feel. Starting your praise with "I" will lead to a sharing of your feelings. "I'm delighted" or "I'm thrilled" are appropriate ways to begin.
- Do it intermittently. Giving praise every time will ensure that the impact diminishes.
- Personalize the praise. Oral feedback is cheap — it costs nothing — and effective. But there are literally hundreds of other ways to show your appreciation: provide a meal voucher, a gift certificate,

time off, or a training course; put a letter in her file; or send a thank-you note to her home.

Negative Feedback

This is something most of us hate giving. It is difficult and, if not done correctly, can lead to further morale problems.

- Immediacy is essential — always deliver feedback as close to the event in question as possible. This enables you to either nip the problem in the bud or ensure that excellence is maintained.
- Make an appointment with your associate to discuss his performance in private. It is essential that he feel like a participant rather than a subject. Don't be afraid to be assertive if he seems unwilling to discuss his performance.
- Get an invitation to provide the feedback. Say "I'd like to discuss the issue with you. Is that OK?" Few people will refuse an opportunity to deal with and remove a stressful situation. And, having accepted your invitation to discuss the issue, your associate will be more open to resolving it.
- Be clear and concise in discussing what you find unacceptable. Providing explicit details of a problem (dates, places, numbers) will avoid giving the impression of a personal attack. Always focus on the specific issue, and avoid sweeping generalizations as to the person's character or work habits. Make it clear that this is an issue of performance, not personality.
- Relate the problem to the larger goals and standards of your company, and be sure that your employee understands the connection. You are not being patronizing — you are treating your associate as an essential participant in the future of the company.
- Confine your comments to areas and issues that your associate can control — if part of the blame or achievement lies elsewhere, acknowledge this.
- Choose your words carefully. Avoid vague generalizations, inflammatory language and exaggerations ("You always do this sort of thing").

- Be specific. Indicate exactly what you are unhappy about ("I'm disappointed that the report was 10 days late").
- Be assertive. Focus on the issue, not the person. Let him know your feelings by using "I" statements whenever possible ("I'm upset because this report does not include the figures we agreed upon"). Also, speak with a firm voice and maintain eye contact.
- Involve your associate in planning for changed behaviour based on this discussion — any solution or continuation of excellence should be seen as a joint venture. Develop a "contract" — either written or spoken — and agree to the terms and to a date by which the provisions of the contract will be fulfilled. The contract should outline key discussion points and the outcomes you have agreed upon. Make sure you both are clear on the meaning of each statement in the contract. Say, as often as necessary: "What I understand this to mean is _____. Do we agree on this?"
- Make another appointment immediately for a future meeting in which the success of the contract can be evaluated. Be clear that you view this as an ongoing process, and are paying attention. You will not forget about this, and neither should your associate.

Each time you need to give negative feedback, run through the following checklist:

1. Get agreement to deal with the issue.
2. Make an appointment for a private discussion.
3. State the facts.
4. Confirm that the issue is a problem.
5. Determine the cause.
6. Ask for a solution. Listen and probe for an acceptable solution.
7. Determine the next step.
8. Write up a contract. Agree on all points and a timeline for implementation.
9. Set a time for the next appointment.

Handling Conflict Between Associates

It's better to debate a question without settling it, than to settle it without debating it.

JOSEPH JOUBERT (1754–1824), FRENCH ESSAYIST

C onflict about ideas can promote creativity and innovation, but conflict between people leads to stress, demoralization and low productivity. Often, you will be called upon to mediate and help resolve conflicts between associates on your team. Here are a few hints:

Assess the problem.

- Is the conflict serious? Is it adversely affecting productivity, service to the team's customers or the project? If not, then leave it alone.
- Can your colleagues solve it on their own, in an appropriate length of time? If they can, encourage them to do so and stay out of it. This will promote personal responsibility. Be sure to praise the conflicting parties if they have resolved their difficulties in a timely and appropriate manner.
- Encourage the parties to listen, try to see the other's point of view and focus on common goals and interests.
- Check back to see if any progress has been made. Point out that you perceive the conflict as a disadvantage for the team as a whole and stress the need for a mutually acceptable solution. Add that if the parties cannot come to a resolution of their differences, you are available to mediate the situation.

Set up a mediation meeting.

- Hold the meeting in a neutral place and at a time when the office will not be buzzing about the meeting.

- Set up the meeting room so that both parties are facing you and a flipchart rather than each other.
- Get down to business as soon as both parties have arrived. Describe how you intend to run the meeting and get their agreement on the process.
- Establish ground rules. All participants are to show respect for one another by not speaking over each other, genuinely attempting to understand the other points of view, sticking to facts rather than personal attacks and being open to compromise.
- Emphasize your role are a neutral mediator, and state the consequences to the team and the parties in conflict if the problem is not solved. You don't have to bully anybody — simply point out that the combatants are damaging the team as a whole.
- Summarize the circumstances as you understand them, and don't take sides. Establish a goal for the meeting that both parties can agree upon.
- Let each party state his or her position in turn, without interruptions, introducing documentation when available and appropriate. Record these ideas on a flipchart. At the end of each statement, recap the main ideas on the flipchart, making sure everybody understands and agrees with the premises.
- When both parties have spoken, post the main ideas on the wall. Ask each party to summarize the sentiments of the other party. Ask them to identify the key issues. Make sure these are factual, not personal, issues. Summarize the main points of conflict and ask for confirmation from those involved.
- Seek suggestions for resolution from the participants first. If none are forthcoming, offer some suggestions yourself. Use humour as appropriate (you could propose an inherently silly solution — such as a game of tiddlywinks to determine who is in the right — to relieve some of the tension).
- Write proposed solutions down next to the issues they address and ask for concrete suggestions as to how these solutions could be carried out and specific dates by which you can expect to see

results. Get everybody's buy-in on these measures and dates. Make sure there is no confusion or fudging going on.

- Where appropriate, commend participants on their openness and honesty.
- Write up the issues, solutions, actions and dates in a memo and circulate it to the participants. Make it clear that you are keeping an eye on the conflict.
- Follow up. Set up another meeting within a reasonably short period of time to review progress. Praise the parties if they are resolving the conflict and implementing the solutions discussed, and assure them that you are on their side and are available for support. If no progress has been made, find out why and assertively let the parties know the consequences of not resolving the matter.
- If one or more of the participants in the conflict continues to be obstructive and seems averse to resolving the issue, notify him or her that you will begin the disciplinary process and proceed to do so.

Preventing Conflict

A fault is a crack, gradually widening and separating people.

CARL JUNG (1875–1961)

*T*here's no avoiding conflict. It is a natural part of teamwork. In fact, when people challenge the status quo or debate how to work better, conflict can be healthy.

When conflict arises because individuals are challenging each other, however, it can undermine everyone's ability to work. Here are some ways you can reduce unhealthy conflict:

- Stick to the facts. Separate and ignore the rumours and bad feelings created by thorny issues.
- Listen to the concerns, interests and goals of others when you consider making changes.
- Communicate on a regular basis. Be open about your plans and thoughts, to reduce potential suspicion or hostility.
- Deal with issues that are hard to face. When touchy issues are ignored, they tend to intensify.
- Quickly resolve issues that block work and threaten deadlines.
- Encourage healthy conflict — that which relates to ideas and changes. Discourage interpersonal conflict, which challenges an individual's power or control.
- Let people know how conflict will be dealt with when it arises.
- Keep your ear to the ground, so you are aware of issues that may become disruptive *before* they get blown out of proportion.
- Set ground rules for your team. Teammates don't have to like each other, but they must co-operate and respect each other.

PART V

Human Resource Management

Health and Safety

*T*he health and safety of your staff is as important as the happiness of your customer. As a manager, you have the legal and moral responsibility to ensure that the workplace is safe and that people's health is not in jeopardy. Here are some ideas for keeping the workplace safe:

- Make health and safety a top priority. Let your people know how you feel about the subject and what your mutual obligations are.
- Unsafe practices should be dealt with immediately. Make no exceptions. Allowing them to continue simply sets a dangerous precedent.
- Involve your people in finding ways to improve.
- Find new and better ways of ensuring safety, even if you have the best record around. Keep yourself knowledgeable about current legislation and your role and responsibility.
- Always assume that what can happen will happen. Be pro-active. Anticipate possible accidents and prioritize them in terms of probability and severity. Establish guidelines for dealing with accidents.
- Post health and safety rules in a prominent place. Keep information up to date.
- Share responsibility for health and safety with your team. Appoint a co-ordinator who can ensure peers maintain safe practices. This person may serve on a health and safety committee.
- Spread ownership for health and safety issues by getting your workers to present a short topic at each meeting. Your encouragement plus a prize for the best presentation might act as an incentive.

- Meet regularly with your people to review statistics and procedures.
- Beware of fatigue caused by excessive work demands. Fatigue reduces people's concentration and makes them more vulnerable to accidents. People can fall asleep or make mistakes that might otherwise not happen.
- Train people in the proper and safe methods of using machinery and equipment. If hazards are high, training needs to be thorough. Procedures should be documented and properly enforced.
- Keep the environment as safe as possible and maintain good housekeeping practices: repair damaged flooring, improve inadequate lighting and replace poorly constructed furniture.
- Review near accidents. They are danger signals.
- Report and record all accidents, no matter how small. These statistics will help you analyze trends, pinpoint problems and confirm the results of corrective actions.
- Always have on staff an adequate number of people with current first-aid certification.
- Make sure people use appropriate safety protection, but remember that protective gear is a last defence against injury, not a replacement for safety. Always stop work when conditions are hazardous.
- Encourage a team approach. Reward and recognize people for taking care of one another.
- Don't let new employees start work until they are fully briefed on your health and safety rules. Make them sign a statement that they understand the rules and undertake to abide by them.

Accidents

egislation in all Western countries requires that employers safeguard the health, safety, and welfare of their staffs, insofar as this may be reasonable and practical. Employees should take care of themselves and others, and co-operate with their employers on matters of health and safety. While your first task is to prevent accidents, here is what you should do if they occur:

- Check whether there is risk of further injuries. If so, clear the area. Instruct people to vacate the building if necessary.
- Assess the nature of the accident. Evaluate whether you are capable of dealing with the injury.
- If the injury is serious, call for emergency assistance. While you are waiting for help,
  - ✓ keep the injured person warm and quiet
  - ✓ be reassuring
  - ✓ do not show that you are afraid or overly concerned
  - ✓ keep the area around the injured as quiet as possible
- If the injury is minor, send the associate for appropriate first aid. Someone in your organization must be trained in these procedures and must be available at all times.
- The Workers' Compensation Board laws of each state require that an associate who is injured on the job or who contracts an occupational disease be furnished reasonable and necessary medical care and be compensated for time lost due to such injury or illness, under specific conditions.
- When an associate is injured on the job or develops a job-related occupational illness:
  - ✓ The associate should be referred to his or her supervisor or department head. First aid will be rendered.

✓ If the injury is serious, the associate will be referred to a nearby medical facility, as determined by management. The department head or supervisor should accompany the associate.

✓ The supervisor will complete an incident report and investigation and forward such reports to the appropriate senior manager, or the general manager, within twenty-four hours of the injury or report of the illness.

✓ The senior manager or designate will complete any forms, as required by state law, and forward all the necessary information to the appropriate enforcement agency, insurance carrier, and a designated head-office official of the organization.

- Any accident which results in death or severe injury requiring medical treatment of five or more persons must be reported to OSHA in addition to the Workers' Compensation Review Board and the corporate human resources office.

- Any call, contact, or communication by or from a representative of the state's Board of Workers' Compensation should be referred immediately to an appropriate senior manager. No statement or document will be furnished to such representative without prior authorization of the designated senior manager, who, in turn, may consult with internal health and safety experts and the organization's insurance carrier.

- On occasion, a supervisor will be requested to attend Workers' Compensation hearings as a witness. This is paid time. At such hearings, the supervisor will need to report on such things as:

✓ how the injury occurred
✓ when it happened
✓ details of treatment provided
✓ the injured person's name and address
✓ your organization's name and address
✓ the name and address of the attending physician

Delays in the submission of your documentation will delay payments to the injured worker.

Anger Management

Did you ever notice how difficult it is to argue with someone who is not obsessed about being right?

WAYNE W. DYER, PSYCHOTHERAPIST
AND BESTSELLING AUTHOR

*H*uman beings experience hindering emotions all the time, from impatience to outright rage. They can be seen on highways (road rage), on the hockey rink and in our homes and places of work. In extreme cases they can lead to physical injury and even death. Our challenge is to harness our emotions so that they are focused on productive endeavours.

Sometimes we confuse hindering emotions with injurious actions — for example, anger with aggression. But emotions can be expressed in different ways, many of them constructive.

Here are some strategies to help you deal more effectively with hindering emotions:

When You Are Angry

- Understand how you are using your anger. Is it being used to
  - ✓ communicate feelings of hurt?
  - ✓ correct the situation?
  - ✓ prevent recurrence?
  - ✓ mend the relationship by improving communications?
- Don't be passive. This is a form of denial. Don't make such statements as "It's OK" or "Don't worry about me," when it really isn't OK.
- Avoid aggressive behaviour. This may be physical — throwing

things, banging your fists or hitting — or verbal — sarcasm or abusive language.

- Don't be passive-aggressive. This results when you bury hindering emotions and express them indirectly (for example, someone who resents cooking burns a meal on purpose). Other symptoms include lateness and "malicious obedience" (following instructions to the letter and screwing up in the process).
- Don't fall into the "triangle syndrome" (venting to someone else rather than to the offending person directly, hinting, placating or avoiding responsibility).
- Be assertive. Focus on getting your own needs met. Also, focus on issues, not on people. If you're not sure of the fine line between assertiveness and aggression, see Assertiveness, page 17.
- Find the trigger. When does anger, frustration, impatience or another hindering emotion rear its head? Do you associate it with a particular person, project or time of day?
- Find the source. This is often different from the trigger. If a project is stalling because it was badly planned from the outset, your anger may still focus on a team member or the supervisor who assigned the task (the trigger), rather than on the concrete cause.
- "Take 10" to chart out your trigger(s) and source(s). Be truthful with yourself — sometimes the source of frustration lies outside the workplace, and you are experiencing the emotion in the environment where you feel you have the most control.
- Focus on the action. Even when a person is the source of your impatience or anger, it will have been an action (or several actions) of theirs that set it off. Find the action.
- Calm down. When hindering emotions boil over, remove yourself either mentally or physically and cool down. Take deep breaths and count to whatever number is necessary, or walk away (remember to excuse yourself first) until you can discuss the precipitating action in a rational manner. Try writing down what is wrong.
- Moderate your memo. If you are documenting a problem for

others, don't rant. Write down your concerns (focus on the source and the actions) in point form, and let the document sit for a day. If possible, get an objective colleague to read the memo before you send it.

- Keep communicating. Many people avoid conflict by withdrawal of one type or another. Typical strategies include pretending there is nothing wrong, sulking and finding distractions. The longer you keep communications open, the better the chance that the issue will be resolved.

- Understand and master your anger. How much control do you have over a situation? Can you change what makes you angry? If you can't, inform someone who can change it (where possible) and let your hindering emotions go. Use humour — if you can laugh (and make other people laugh) at a situation, you can defuse it.

When Others Are Angry

- Listen. Allow the person to be angry or frustrated. Meet him as an equal. If he is sitting, sit. If he is standing, stand.

- Don't interrupt. Make sure she says everything she wants to say, and prompt her non-verbally when necessary.

- Show empathy. Hindering emotions are a natural reaction to difficult situations — your task is to identify the problem he is facing and help him deal with it.

- Clarify her position. Relate to actions and specific issues, not personalities and generalities. Confirm with her that you have understood her position.

- Don't patronize or provoke him.

- Pace her. Use a quiet, moderate tone and restrained gestures. This will calm her down, since continuing to be frustrated requires as much energy from others as it does from you.

- Pinpoint and plan. Identify the issues and work with him on a plan to solve them. Get it in writing. If the problem is a complex or recurring one, get him to document it and work with you towards a solution.

Chemical Abuse

Drunkenness is the ruin of reason. It is prema-
ture old age. It is temporary death.

St. Basil (330–79), Greek religious leader

A buse of drugs and alcohol in the workplace is a monumental problem. And anyone can be an addict, from your CEO to your front-line worker. Here are practical ideas about what you can do:

- Communicate regularly with your people. Be aware of the following symptoms of abuse:
  - ✓ excessive absenteeism, particularly on Mondays
  - ✓ regular tardiness
  - ✓ declining productivity
  - ✓ increased injuries and accidents
  - ✓ personal problems — legal, financial or family
  - ✓ constant and/or suspicious phone calls
  - ✓ physical deterioration such as slurred speech, runny nose, scratching and dry skin
  - ✓ changes in interactions with others
  - ✓ increased isolation from or conflict with peers
  - ✓ rebellious behaviour towards authority
  - ✓ erratic behaviour, mood swings, disorientation
  - ✓ more frequent washroom visits
- When you think there's a problem, you should
  - ✓ prepare to deal with it assertively
  - ✓ document signs and obvious patterns
- Never
  - ✓ enable the person to get away with poor job performance

- ✓ ignore or excuse unacceptable behaviour
- ✓ take on the person's responsibilities
- ✓ make excuses to others, cover up the problem, pick up the slack or fill in for them
- ✓ feel responsible
- ✓ try to solve problems you are not qualified to solve
- Confront the person with your evidence. This should be done privately and in a supportive manner (see Counselling, page 135). In your discussion you should:
  - ✓ Avoid blaming, using guilt tactics or getting sidetracked with the associate's personal problems. Stick to work issues.
  - ✓ Refer the associate to a professional to deal with personal problems. An Employee Assistance Program is geared to deal with these issues.
  - ✓ Clarify goals and standards. The person should refocus on what is expected of him.
  - ✓ Let the person know the consequences of poor performance.
- If performance does not improve, follow disciplinary steps according to company policy.
- If you are unionized, enlist your union representative's support in your actions, be they disciplinary or focused on rehabilitation.

Stress

The bow too tensely strung is easily broken.

SYRUS PUBLILIUS (1ST CENTURY B.C.)

S tress is a major cause of work absenteeism and a host of social problems. Stress is unique to each person. A few of the most common causes are lack of control over one's work life, moving, and difficulties in a relationship. Here are some things you can do to reduce your stress:

- Accept the fact that stress is a natural part of modern life. Some stress can even be positive since it increases the body's production of adrenaline, which generates energy.
- Identify the things you enjoy doing most and that take your mind off stressful situations. Build more of these activities into your daily routine.
- Break up your working day so that you have time to refresh yourself. Make a point of getting away from your desk to clear your head and recharge your batteries.
- Get as much exercise as possible. The better you feel about your body, and the better shape your body is in, the better you will feel mentally.
- Establish a relationship with a good listener. When you are close to your boiling point, talk through your frustrations with your confidant. Talking will relieve the pressure. Bottling up your problems can cause mental and physical illness.
- Say the Serenity Prayer to yourself if you are frustrated about something you cannot change:

God grant me the serenity to accept the things I cannot change,
the courage to change the things I can, and the wisdom to know the
difference.

- Find an outside interest or hobby. The time spent on this activity will give you a mental break.
- Experiment with your diet. Eliminate foods that contain caffeine, which can increase your tension. Sugar before bed reduces your ability to sleep.
- Learn to manage your time effectively (see Time Management, page 39). Continuously fighting the clock is a losing battle. You must change your habits and generate more free time to relax or do the things you want to do.
- Don't use medication, drugs or alcohol to ease the problem. These substances temporarily mask the problem without solving it. You must remove the causes of your problem.
- Meditate once or twice a day, or as needed, for 10 to 20 minutes. To achieve this relaxed state:
  ✓ Focus on a pleasant image or word.
  ✓ Close your eyes and lie or sit in a comfortable position.
  ✓ Consciously relax all your muscles by focusing on each from your head to your toes, allowing your body to "sink."
  ✓ Breathe slowly and naturally; imagine a pleasant scene or repeat a key word to yourself.
  ✓ Don't worry about your technique.
  ✓ Refocus and put other thoughts out of your mind.
- Learn to say no when others' demands are overloading your time and ability.
- Delegate more of your workload (see Delegating, page 143) so that you will have more time to think and plan. Typical tasks to delegate include
  ✓ routine items
  ✓ data collection
  ✓ some meetings

IDENTIFYING BURNOUT SYMPTOMS

Waiting until you become incapacitated from stress is extremely harmful. So here's a quick test to check your need to take corrective action (check off your response):

	Yes	No
• Are you becoming preoccupied with your own thoughts when in the company of others, so that you find it hard to follow or engage in meaningful discussions?	❏	❏
• Is it difficult to shake off minor illnesses such as coughs and colds?	❏	❏
• Are you becoming ill more often than you used to?	❏	❏
• Are you seeing less of your family and friends than you used to?	❏	❏
• Are you increasingly short-tempered with people?	❏	❏
• Do you become more irritable in company than you used to?	❏	❏
• Are you working longer hours but not accomplishing more?	❏	❏
• Are you missing deadlines and appointments without realizing it?	❏	❏
• Do you tire easily?	❏	❏
• Have you stopped or cut back on your recreational or leisure activities and hobbies?	❏	❏

A score of more than seven Yes responses suggests that you should put into practice the ideas on managing stress.

Harassment

The first step in the evolution of ethics is a
sense of solidarity with other human beings.
ALBERT SCHWEITZER (1875–1965), FRENCH THEOLOGIAN,
PHILOSOPHER, PHYSICIAN AND MUSIC SCHOLAR

*H*arassment is behaviour that is unwelcome. Harassment can take many forms, and can be based on many things, including, but not limited to, ethnic or national origin, sex, sexual orientation, marital status, age or creed. Contrary to common belief, harassment can and does exist when unreported, and it does not go away by itself. People in positions of authority, including managers and union representatives, are held legally accountable if they fail to act in an appropriately swift and decisive manner to counter workplace harassment. So what can you do?

- First, familiarize yourself with general company policy on harassment. Post that policy in a visible place in your department and provide copies of it to your associates.
- If your company has an educational video on forms of harassment, encourage your team to watch it during business hours.
- Have on hand pamphlets or literature dealing with harassment. Do not worry that you are giving your employees tools to use against you — you are empowering them.
- Be a model of inclusionary, non-racist, non-sexist behaviour. Use gender-neutral and race-neutral language. Indicate that there is zero tolerance for harassment in your department.

If Someone Comes to You with a Complaint of Harassment

- Deal with the complaint right away, to show that you in no way condone the behaviour.
- Collect the facts swiftly, assertively and with minimum disruption. Find out
  - ✓ what happened
  - ✓ when and where it happened
  - ✓ how often and for how long it has happened
  - ✓ who the alleged harasser is
  - ✓ whether he or she is aware that the behaviour was unwelcome
  - ✓ whether there are witnesses
  - ✓ what other corroborative evidence exists
- Determine the severity of the offence. In the case of sexual harassment, for example, severe punishment (dismissal) is appropriate if the accused can be proved to have based a decision to hire on receiving sexual favours, or if the complainant was implicitly or explicitly threatened with job loss if sexual favours were withheld. Any form of harassment merits penalty if the harassment creates a hostile, offensive or threatening work environment. Be cautious about determining the severity of the offence — if necessary, consult with your superior in the matter, but do not involve anyone else.
- Ensure there is no backlash against the complainant, and keep the complainant's confidentiality wherever possible.

If You Are Harassed

- Confront the harasser and make your feelings known. If an apology is immediately forthcoming and the situation no longer recurs, you can choose to let it slide.
- If the situation recurs or worsens, inform someone in authority immediately and assertively.

Absenteeism

bsenteeism costs everyone. It increases your costs by necessitating the hiring of temporary staff and paying for increased overtime. It reduces your customer service since fill-in staff are less effective. And it aggravates fellow employees who are often called upon to pick up the slack.

You cannot avoid some absenteeism. But levels higher than 10% indicate a serious problem; levels lower than 5% are good. If you have a problem, here's how you can turn it around:

- Keep statistics to pinpoint problems and trends. Your data base should tell you
  - ✓ who was absent
  - ✓ when they were absent
  - ✓ why they were absent
- Compare your area to other similar work areas. Find out if your people are
  - ✓ better than average
  - ✓ average
  - ✓ worse than average
- Analyze your data. Look for applications of the 80/20 principle. You may find that
  - ✓ 20% of your people are absent 80% of the time,
  - ✓ 80% of the absenteeism occurs on 20% of the days, or
  - ✓ 20% of the causes account for 80% of the time off.
- Let your people know that you are aware of and concerned about the problem.
- Ask them to help you identify the most critical causes. See if you can make improvements. Things you can improve include

- ✓ boredom
- ✓ monotony
- ✓ lack of reward
- ✓ lack of challenge
- ✓ lack of responsibility
- ✓ lack of feedback

Items you have little or no control over include

- ✓ personal problems
- ✓ sickness
- ✓ family problems (sick child, bereavement)

- Deal with absenteeism immediately, whether your associate has been away for one day or one month. Interview the person when he or she gets back to find out why. Show your interest and concern.

- Let new associates know your attitude towards absenteeism during orientation as well as the company's policies and procedures. While your approach should not be threatening, people should know that the consequences may be
  - ✓ loss of pay
  - ✓ hostility of peers who have to fill in or do extra work
  - ✓ a note in the person's personnel record
  - ✓ demotion
  - ✓ termination

- Be consistent and follow company guidelines, but show empathy for those who are having a legitimate temporary problem. Work with them to get them back on track.

- Focus your energy on those associates who are responsible for the most absenteeism. Typically, 20% of your people account for 80% of the problem.

Conducting an Attitude Survey

*W*hat are your people thinking? The worse those thoughts are the less likely they will tell you. Discontent with managerial policies, processes and personalities will more often manifest itself in absenteeism, turnover and shoddy job performance. These are all symptoms of an underlying disease, and can only be dealt with after a thorough diagnosis — an attitude survey. Attitude surveys, if properly formulated and carried out, will provide you with an accurate assessment of what's wrong (and right) with your team, your division or your company.

Before the Survey

- Research survey methods and sources thoroughly before deciding whether to get outside help or to construct and conduct a survey in-house. Your decision will be based on
  - ✓ cost
  - ✓ reliability (produces similar results again and again)
  - ✓ validity (tracks what it purports to measure)
  - ✓ comprehensiveness (measures a variety of subjects)
- Using an outside resource will have pros and cons. The cons might include costs, but the benefits will include
  - ✓ professional advice
  - ✓ proven surveys
  - ✓ industry benchmark data
  - ✓ sophisticated software that permits manipulation of data for analysis

- ✓ credibility with staff
- ✓ an easily understood feedback package
- ✓ time savings
- ✓ generic or customized surveys
- ✓ confidentiality

Preparing a Survey

- Determine which subjects to measure. For example:
  - ✓ recognition
  - ✓ communications
  - ✓ relationship with boss
  - ✓ confidence in management
  - ✓ career development
  - ✓ job satisfaction
  - ✓ training and career opportunities
  - ✓ compensation and benefits
- Decide whether to collect information with open- or closed-ended questions. The latter are typically scored with a Likert scale, which has five possible responses:
  - ✓ strongly disagree
  - ✓ disagree
  - ✓ neither agree nor disagree
  - ✓ agree
  - ✓ strongly agree
- Set a date for conducting the survey. In order to get the highest level of participation, conduct the survey in-house, during work hours. Surveys rarely take more than 45 minutes.
- Tell your employees in advance — a week's notice should be sufficient. Assure them of the professional and beneficial nature of the survey through direct communication, possibly in small face-to-face "information sessions." These sessions should cover
  - ✓ the survey's purpose, its process and the manner in which the accumulated data will be used and disseminated,

- ✓ the date, time and place of the survey — this allows employees to arrange their schedules so they can participate without falling behind in their work,
- ✓ the safeguards in place to protect confidentiality and anonymity, and
- ✓ when and how employees can access to the survey's results.
- Reassure your employees that the results of the survey will be made available to them and will be used to make operational changes in a forthright manner. Emphasize that this is about correcting problems and recognizing efficient processes, and not about individual witch-hunting.

During the Survey

- Use a quiet, appropriately sized meeting room or schedule people throughout the day if the sample is large.
- Before the survey begins, explain why you are conducting it and how to complete it. Allow time for questions. Emphasize that the process is voluntary. If people are not convinced about the benefit or confidentiality, allow them to exclude themselves by leaving or spoiling their questionnaire.
- Seat people a reasonable distance apart so that they cannot see others' responses.
- Give people ample time to complete the survey. Allow them to leave when finished. Thank them for participating.

After the Survey

- Analyze the data. Develop graphs to show highlights, trends and comparisons.
- Review the results with management. Plan to share the information with staff. Decide
  - ✓ how to communicate the information
  - ✓ when it will be done
  - ✓ what information to provide

- Communicate results of the survey to all employees in a format that they can easily understand. A personal presentation with charts and graphs should be supplemented with a written summary.
- Develop plans for improvement with employees' input.
- Continue to improve morale by solving new problems as they arise, so that people will see that you are sincere about dealing with their concerns. Evaluate your success when you next do a survey, one year after the first.
- Conduct focus groups with staff where clarification is needed or where there is value in defining the problems specific to a particular department. Consider using a nonpartisan facilitator to get the most useful information.

Hiring Interviews

Better the devil you know than the devil you don't know.

ANONYMOUS

*H*iring the wrong person for the job can poison an entire department (not to mention its budget for training and severance), while hiring the right person can boost everyone's morale and productivity. To get the best fit of person to placement, you must master the art of the hiring interview. The best interview is structured much like a meeting — an opening to set the agenda, information gathering (from both you and the interviewee) and a solid conclusion. And, just as for a meeting, you should prepare beforehand and evaluate afterward.

Preparation

- Refamiliarize yourself with the job, environment and skills you are looking for.
- Review the candidate's resumé. Identify key issues that need clarification or confirmation.
- Arrange the furnishings in your office or meeting room to promote open discussion. Sit next to or facing the candidate in comfortable chairs. Sitting behind a desk will distance you from the candidate.
- Bring writing materials so you can make notes on important issues. Don't rely on your memory, particularly if you have a number of interviews back to back.
- Consider interviewing with a colleague who can add insight and objectivity to the process. A second person can also help write

notes while you ask the questions, or vice versa; after all, it's difficult to make extensive notes while you are listening.

- Schedule enough time between appointments to evaluate each interviewee and document your thoughts. If you do not do this, it will be difficult to make an accurate assessment of each candidate. Preliminary interviews can last as long as an hour; final interviews, two hours.

Opening

- Welcome interviewees with a smile and a handshake. Introduce yourself and any other co-interviewers.
- Start the interview by describing the agenda and how much time you expect the meeting will run. Your opening comment might be, "First I'd like to learn more about you, then we'll discuss the position, and I'll tell you more about the company. Finally, I will try and answer any questions you may have. This should take us about an hour." Letting candidates know how much time you have allotted will reassure them that they will have the opportunity to give their information and time to ask key questions.
- Avoid making a judgement too early in the interview. Premature judging will show your inability to listen and to be objective.

Information Gathering

- Get to know the applicant. Use her resumé, the job application she filled out, and any preliminary material she may have submitted to formulate questions and draw out her professional history.
- Ask open-ended, specific questions to generate non-canned responses. For example, ask "Give me one example of how you disciplined an employee," then ask why, how, and what the result was. This will give you an indication of the candidate's ability to think clearly, solve problems and communicate effectively and concisely.

- Note his body language (see Reading Body Language, page 54). Pay special attention to inappropriate attire, symptoms of anxiety or prevarication (often around inexplicable gaps in employment history and references) or, conversely, evidence of enthusiasm and interest (leaning forward, nodding). Make sure you take cultural differences into account.
- Analyze her resumé. Since most people today have professionally prepared resumés, be on the watch for inflated or generalized job descriptions and accomplishments, gaps in employment history, missing references, etc. and ask probing questions about items you find questionable.
- Proceed logically. Plan your questions so that one topic leads to another, and take notes. Don't jump from topic to topic — this will confuse the candidate and limit the amount of information you extract.
- Allow candidates time to answer questions. Silence will draw most people to speak. If you must prompt him to answer, repeat his last relevant statement as a question in a neutral tone. For example, "I missed work once or twice a month" can be met with "Once or twice a month?" to elicit more information.
- Instead of asking leading questions, describe potentially challenging on-the-job situations and ask the candidate how she would handle them. Request specific ideas. Best of all, get the candidate to describe how she handled a similar situation in the past. If she resorts to generalizations or clichés, request that she elaborate in more specific terms.
- Remember: the law prohibits questions about
  ✓ race
  ✓ religion
  ✓ country of birth
  ✓ criminal history
  ✓ age
  ✓ marital status

✓ sexual orientation
✓ financial status

- Give information back. Take the candidate through the job description, the department and organizational culture and your expectations. Allow him to decide whether he is suited to or interested in the position as described.

Information Giving

- After gathering the relevant information from the candidate you should discuss the job. Describe the tasks and criteria for success so the candidate can decide whether or not the job suits her.
- Describe the company, its culture and your expectations regarding the position. Don't spend too much time selling the company — leave time for questions.

Closing

- Outline the hiring process for the candidate. If there are second-round interviews, deadlines to fill the position, or other complicating factors (such as a seniority clause in a union-shop contract), mention them now.
- Be honest. If the candidate isn't right for the position, say so. Don't string him along. Try to be diplomatic without provoking hopes that won't materialize. If the candidate's qualifications are good, but not right for the specific position, tell him you will keep his resumé on file in case another, more suitable position opens up.

Immediately after the Interview

Evaluate the candidate right away. If your organization has a standard form with which to assess a candidate, use it directly after the interview to record your immediate impressions. If not, make a brief note evaluating the candidate's

✓ background/education/employment history
✓ skills/attributes

✓ job suitability

✓ presence/voice/mannerisms

✓ appearance

Checking References

- Conduct a thorough reference check of your shortlisted candidates. Discard personal friends and relatives, who will offer biased opinions. Focus on the candidate's former boss, peers, subordinates and customers (internal or external).
- If candidates have professional qualifications, ask for transcripts. If these are not available, check their credentials with the institutions that awarded their degrees, diplomas or designations.
- Confirm information from candidates' resumés and interviews regarding
  - ✓ dates of employment
  - ✓ positions held
  - ✓ accuracy of special claims and achievements
  - ✓ competence
  - ✓ circumstances under which they left
- Ask open-ended questions:
  - ✓ What are the candidate's strengths?
  - ✓ What are the candidate's weaknesses?
  - ✓ What was her most important contribution to your organization?
  - ✓ What will you miss most about him?
  - ✓ How do you feel about her decision to leave?
  - ✓ Can you describe his relationship with boss/peers/subordinates?
- Ask follow-up questions where appropriate. For example, "Can you explain that?" or "Can you tell me more?" or "Could you give me an example?"
- Confirm any hunches you developed in your interview.
- Finally, ask if there are any questions that the referee thinks you should have asked.

Generic Questions You Can Ask

- If you got the job, what action would you take in the first month?
- How would you deal with a 10% budget reduction?
- What do you like least about your existing job? Why?
- What do you like most about your existing job? Why?
- Who was the best boss you had? Why?
- Who was your worst boss? Why?
- In what way do you and your boss think alike? In what way do you differ?
- What is the most difficult thing about your existing job? Why?
- What are your career goals? How do you plan to get there?
- What is your major achievement in your last job? Tell me how you accomplished it.
- How do you react when you get negative feedback?
- Give an example of how you disciplined an employee. What was the result?
- What was the lowest point of your job? What happened? How did you deal with it?
- If you have one major weakness, what is it? What steps are you taking to improve?
- If I were to ask your last boss to describe you in five words, what would he or she say?
- As I am going to interview other candidates, what would you like me to remember about you in relation to this position?

INTERVIEW CHECKLIST

	Yes	No
• Were you prepared?	❏	❏
• Did you set up the room to promote an open discussion?	❏	❏
• Did you describe the steps you wanted to follow to the interviewee?	❏	❏
• Did you listen most of the time?	❏	❏
• Did you withhold judgement?	❏	❏
• Did you probe sufficiently?	❏	❏
• Was your language and questioning free of any bias?	❏	❏
• Did you pick up and respond to nonverbal clues?	❏	❏
• Did you let the candidate know what to expect after the interview?	❏	❏
• Were you able to gather all the information you need to make a decision (excluding reference)?	❏	❏

Learn from any negative answers and improve your next interview.

Orientation

*H*aving hired the right people, you can promote their successful adjustment to the organization by orienting them properly.

Before Arrival

- Plan to ensure a successful integration of the new person:
  - ✓ Have the work station set up with supplies.
  - ✓ Have someone greet the new employee on arrival.
  - ✓ Post a letter on the bulletin board welcoming the employee and inviting others to do the same.

The First Day

- Spend some quiet time getting to know your new associates. Learn about their work backgrounds, previous jobs, likes and dislikes.
- Give the associates documentation on salary and benefits.
- Give new employees a tour of the facilities. Show them the key facilities, including parking, washrooms, the cafeteria and emergency exits.
- Review the company's mission, values and philosophy if these are available and documented. Discuss how new employees can contribute to the successful achievement of corporate goals.
- Show them each department and how they relate to yours. Also show the major products and services. Information will give people the big picture so they can see how they fit into it.
- While you can do some of the orientation, consider involving someone else. Pairing the new associate with a person from another work area can be beneficial in that it

- ✓ suggests that departments work together
- ✓ stresses teamwork
- ✓ establishes contacts with people in other areas
- ✓ improves communications between work areas
- ✓ demonstrates your esteem for people outside your work area
- To facilitate the associate's integration into the social fabric of the company, provide a "buddy" who can act as a mentor when you are not available and be company during breaks.

Later

- Do not prejudice the associate about other people or departments by running them down. Allow new employees to form their own opinions based on their experience.
- Establish an open-door policy so that the associate has easy access to you when needed.
- Follow up regularly to see how new associates are doing. Praise their accomplishments. This will increase their confidence and sense of satisfaction at having joined the organization.
- Treat new associates as a resource. They will have a fresh perspective on different ways of doing things. Be receptive to their input by showing your interest and, when possible, acting on their suggestions.
- Schedule a meeting about six weeks after the orientation to find out
  - ✓ how the person is doing
  - ✓ what more you can do to help
  - ✓ new ways of improving the orientation process
- Consider inviting a person's family or significant other for an orientation. You will demonstrate your interest in the person.

ORIENTATION CHECKLIST

Use this list to ensure your new associate gets off on the right foot:

- Prepare work station ❑
- Explain corporate mission, vision and values ❑
- Review company policies (including health and safety) ❑
- Review benefit program ❑
- Give copies of rules, benefits, policies ❑
- Review the union contract (if applicable) ❑
- Introduce to work peers ❑
- Conduct, or have someone else conduct, tour ❑
- Introduce to key contacts in other departments ❑
- Identify emergency exits, washrooms, cafeteria ❑
- Demonstrate products and services ❑
- Introduce to "buddy" ❑
- Set up training program — technical and soft skills ❑

Training

*Learning is like a magic carpet that transports
you to new enlightenment and understanding.*

SALLY FIELD, ACTRESS

*T*raining is a lot cheaper than ignorance. On-the-job training in technical, interpersonal, team and business skills is a key component of any manager's duties. Here are some ideas to help:

- Establish career and organization goals for each person in your area. This information will give you an idea of how much time you need to devote to the development of each person. Those with the highest ambitions and those with the lowest level of skills will require the most training.
- Determine what kind of training to give. There are many ways to train people:
  - ✓ **Job rotation** will give your associate a wider perspective and additional job skills.
  - ✓ **Cross training** enables people to substitute for one another during temporary absences.
  - ✓ **Task forces** and other temporary problem-solving groups allow members to learn more about a performance improvement topic.
  - ✓ **Delegation** of additional responsibilities enables people to learn more challenging tasks and increase their opportunities to demonstrate managerial talent.
  - ✓ **Workshops**, on-site or at public seminars, allow people to learn from an expert.

- ✓ **Mentoring** enhances the skills of associates by exposing them to someone other than their immediate boss who has that skill-set.
- ✓ **Conferences** and other industry-specific meetings will enable the associate to network and access information about their industry or profession.
- ✓ **Computer-based training** will enable a self-directed learner to acquire skills, step-by-step, on a computer, learning at her own pace.
- ✓ **Distance courses**, including Internet-based programs, are also ideal for self-directed learners. These programs enable the associate to learn outside of business hours at his own pace (see "Checklist for Choosing an Online Training Program" on the next page).

- Ensure that associates get feedback on their progress. This feedback can be from you or a peer or through self-evaluation.
- When training people yourself, walk the associate through four steps:
  1. Explain the task, why it needs to be done and how it should be done.
  2. Demonstrate the task. If the task is long and complex, break it down into bite-size modules and sequences, doing one part at a time.
  3. Ask trainees to try the task while you observe them. Note things that they do well as well as mistakes.
  4. Finally, give the trainees feedback. Praise any progress to increase their confidence. Be specific about what they did well.
- In the event that you notice a mistake, review your instructions through description and demonstration. Ask trainees to confirm their understanding of the task before trying it again.
- If you have demonstrated a task more than three times and the trainee is unable to learn the task, consider breaking the task down even further. If this cannot be done, or has already been done, it is likely that your trainee is not suited for the job.

- Establish the trainee's preferred method of learning. Some people learn best by hearing, others by seeing and a third group by doing. If it is difficult to decide which is the trainee's preferred method, or if you are training more than one person, use all three instruction methods.

CHECKLIST FOR CHOOSING AN ONLINE TRAINING PROGRAM

Before buying an e-learning program, test its effectiveness against these criteria:

Does the program
- ✓ Work effectively at the speed your computer operates? You don't want to have to spend hundreds of dollars upgrading your computer for just one new application.
- ✓ Provide excellent content, or does it focus on glitzy? Avoid programs that mask poor content with great design.
- ✓ Have an easy-to-follow site map that enables you to jump directly to the point you want? Or do you need to go through a variety of tedious iterations to get to your starting point?
- ✓ Require only a few clicks to start the program? Each click will add to your frustration as you wait for additional downloading of new data.
- ✓ Have an 800 number to call in the event of problems using the program?
- ✓ Require few or no additional plug-ins or software, which might be difficult to obtain?

Workshops

Give a man a fish and you feed him for a day.
Teach a man to fish and he will be fed for the
rest of his life.

CHINESE PROVERB

A s a manager, you have skills that can be transferred to others. An effective way to teach others is to run a workshop.

Planning the Session

- Time your training so that it is not too early or too late. If you time your session too far in advance of when people need to use the skills, they will forget them. Training after they have started will require some unlearning since they may have developed bad habits.
- Ask yourself whether the training will benefit your customers — internal or external. If not, don't waste your time and the organization's money.
- Determine whether people need knowledge or skills, or both. If skills are needed, you will need to incorporate practice into your workshop.
- Plan short sessions. People will retain skills more effectively if you divide training into half-day lesson modules.
- Consider buying a packaged program if your development costs are high. Avoid packages that
  - ✓ cannot be customized
  - ✓ have audio-visuals from a very different industry
  - ✓ are aimed at a very different audience level
  - ✓ are made in a foreign country

- Find out about your trainees. You should know
  - ✓ which previous courses they have taken
  - ✓ what they need to know
  - ✓ what they need to do better
  - ✓ their motivation level
  - ✓ their literacy level
- Develop materials to suit the audience. For example, materials for people with poor literacy should have more pictures and diagrams.
- Materials will be better if they
  - ✓ contain one idea per page
  - ✓ are written in simple language
  - ✓ have lots of space to make notes
  - ✓ are interactive — have spaces for people to write answers, do quizzes and complete checklists
- Book meeting rooms early. Advise attendees of location. Provide maps if necessary.

Before the Session

- Get to the training room early. Check your equipment.
- Arrange seating to suit the purpose of the session. Use
  - ✓ theatre style for a show and tell
  - ✓ U-shaped for interactive training
  - ✓ round tables for teamwork exercises
- Mingle with participants to establish rapport.

At the Start of the Session

- Begin on a high note. Memorize the opening to start off strongly and set the tone for the workshop or get a senior manager to start the workshop off.
- Develop a contract at the onset about what you expect of participants and what they can expect of you. Remind them that
  - ✓ they are responsible for their own learning
  - ✓ they should let you know if their needs are not being met

- ✓ you will be starting and finishing on time
- Also, let people know about
  - ✓ fire exits
  - ✓ telephone availability
  - ✓ washroom locations
  - ✓ break times
- Introduce yourself and get people to introduce themselves or have them interview one another. They can let everyone know their partners'
  - ✓ names
  - ✓ job and special skills
  - ✓ key objectives
  - ✓ concerns about the workshop
- Make the objectives of the program clear. Post them where they can be seen clearly.
- Review the agenda so people are aware of how you aim to achieve your objectives.

During the Session
- Stay on schedule:
  - ✓ Negotiate break lengths with participants.
  - ✓ Note restarting times on the flipchart.
  - ✓ Close the door at the agreed-upon starting time.
  - ✓ Don't wait for stragglers.
  - ✓ Don't summarize for people who come in late.
- If things don't go according to plan, don't raise awareness of the problem by apologizing.
- Don't be afraid to admit you don't have an answer to a question. Ask the others if they have the answer. If not, offer to get back to the person. Don't lie or "wing it." Your integrity and honesty could be compromised and, with it, your ability to influence the audience.
- Avoid using complex words like *parameter*. Such words indicate that you are being theoretical and not down-to-earth.

- Use visuals wherever possible. They are six to eight times more effective than verbal instructions.
- Make sure that diagrams are culturally neutral.
- Stop from time to time to poll the audience. Ask, for example, "How many of you have tried this?" A poll provides a welcome change of pace and gives you useful information.
- Repeat or rephrase questions that are not heard by everyone in the audience.
- Vary the pace and presentation techniques as often as possible to keep interest at a high level. Remember, the attention span of most adults is about seven minutes. So change the tempo and the presentation medium, and intersperse team tasks with individual assignments.
- Never show a video or conduct a lecture immediately after lunch since this is the time when people's energy drops to its lowest level. Instead, schedule a fun activity or some physical exercises.
- Draw information out of the group wherever possible. Their participation provides a change of pace and also validates your ideas in practical terms.
- End your workshop with a challenge. Ask everyone to commit to using some part of the workshop in the next two weeks. Conduct a survey, one person at a time, of what their intentions are.
- Ask people to write their action plans on a sheet of paper. Put these into self addressed envelopes and mail them to participants 60 days after the workshop.

After the Session

- Evaluate your training not by how much people enjoyed your program but by whether they put the skills to use.
- Set up refresher courses, at which time you can confirm the effectiveness of the initial training, reinforce key skills and add some new ones.

Performance Appraisals

*A*n effective appraisal can lead to better performance. Always conduct the appraisal in a problem-solving spirit and focus on the future, not the past. The process should hold no surprises since daily problems should be dealt with immediately.

Preparation
- Update the person's file regularly so that your feedback will be based on facts.
- Set up a meeting time with your associate. Give him enough time to prepare. Don't schedule the meeting for a Friday, especially if a performance problem is going to be discussed.
- Allocate sufficient time. Two hours should allow for a full interchange of ideas.
- Provide the associate with a sample questionnaire, which allows her to do some focused thinking about the process and content of the interview, reduces the probability of surprises and gives her a chance to complete the appropriate form from her perspective.
- Make sure that your documentation is prepared. Review the file so you are familiar with
  - ✓ previous performance goals
  - ✓ the collective agreement (if appropriate)
  - ✓ the job description
  - ✓ special achievements
  - ✓ problems since the last appraisal
- In your preparation, identify new projects, goals and standards that should be achieved in the next period. Be prepared to handle unrealistic goals or those that you cannot support.

Conducting the Appraisal

- Set the climate for a productive interchange. Welcome the employee with a smile.
- Sit in a comfortable position next to the employee rather than behind a desk. This will improve communication.
- Set the ground rules for the meeting. These might include being
  - ✓ open
  - ✓ frank
  - ✓ factual where possible
  - ✓ positive
  - ✓ future-focused
- Ask the associate for concerns about the process. Respond openly and honestly.
- Next, review the associate's job. You may find that your ideas about the nature of the job responsibilities are different. Priorities may have changed. Or maybe your associate's skill set now allows a new dimension to the job.
- Review the goals that were set previously. Have they been achieved? If not, why not? Were problems within or beyond the associate's control?
- Review the associate's achievements. Refer to your file. Also ask about areas where the associate has been effective. Focus on the narrative parts of the evaluation than the numerical ratings.
- Review areas where improvement is needed. Be specific about your concerns. Give examples to illustrate your knowledge and understanding of the issue.
- If your system calls for it, give your overall rating of the employee. If your discussions to this point have been open, frank and factual, the final rating should be no surprise.
- Plan for improvement. Be positive. Ask for ideas to improve weaknesses. If the associate struggles to identify appropriate solutions, suggest some of your own. Gain commitment.
- Set an action plan to ensure that weaknesses are dealt with.

- Deal with the associate's goals and career aspirations. Be honest. Don't make promises that are hard to keep. Opportunities for advancement are all too few in organizations that are downsizing. Focus on development, personal growth and providing opportunities to undertake important new projects, should this be appropriate.
- Before wrapping up, ask for feedback about the process. Is the associate satisfied? Has the meeting met his objectives?
- Finally, summarize the key points of the appraisal and close the meeting on a positive note. Provide a copy of the appraisal to the associate.

Follow-up

- Hold regular formal and informal meetings with your associate to ensure that action plans for improvement are being implemented. Recognize special achievements. If she is not living up to commitments, find out why and help her get back on track (see Giving Feedback, page 154).

Performance Appraisal Checklist

Learn from each evaluation by identifying specific areas of improvement. Spend two to three minutes immediately after the interview to reflect on your performance.

For each of the following statements, rate yourself on a scale of 1 to 10. The higher the number, the more like the characteristic you are. When you have finished, total your scores.

1. I let the associate do most of the talking.
2. I listened to the associate's ideas.
3. I was prepared to suggest solutions to problems and development needs but let the associate contribute first.
4. I did not teach, argue or defend my authority.
5. I recognized positive performance and identified and dealt with problems.
6. I supported the associate's ideas rather than forcing my own.
7. I invited alternatives rather than assuming there is only one way to approach an issue.
8. I used open-ended, reflective and directive questions to stimulate discussion.
9. I was specific and descriptive when I expressed a concern about performance.
10. My associate knows I want him/her to succeed.

Total
90–100   You are leading successful discussions.
70–89   You have significant strengths. A few improvements are needed.
50–69   You have some strengths but a significant number of improvements are needed.
Below 50 Make a serious effort to improve in several categories, especially areas where you scored 6 or less, regardless of your total score.

Discipline Interviews

> *The superior man always remembers how he*
> *was punished for his mistakes. The inferior man*
> *always remembers what presents he got.*
>
> CONFUCIUS (C. 551–479 B.C.)

The discipline interview is one of the most frequently avoided responsibilities of a manager. It brings to a head performance problems that, if not resolved, could lead to suspension or even termination. Here's how you can handle this difficult situation:

Before the Interview

- Prepare yourself thoroughly. Your files should contain documentation detailing specific performance problems, with dates, and a record of previous counselling sessions.
- Keep copies of any written warnings. Include dates, times and rules broken or policies violated.
- In a unionized workplace environment, make sure that you abide by the terms of the collective agreement. If you are not sure of your rights, consult your labour relations expert.
- Invite the employee to a private place for the interview, preferably in neutral territory. In some instances, you may also want to include a recorder. If necessary, ensure that the shop steward is present.

During the Interview

- Get right to the point by explaining the reason for the interview.
- Be specific when describing the problem. Give examples, with dates.

- Ask if the employee shares your observations and concern. The more specifically you have described the problem, the more likely it is she will agree with you.
- Give your associate the opportunity to explain, and listen carefully.
- Ask the associate how he intends to address the issue. Only give suggestions if he has no ideas. Confirm that he has agreed to implement the action and/or change his behaviour.
- Let the associate know what stage in the disciplinary process has been reached: for example, first spoken warning, or second written warning. State that the warning will be in her personnel file and how long it will remain there.
- Discuss the consequences if the problem continues. Again ask for confirmation of understanding.
- If termination is the next step, it should be noted in the last written report. For example, "If this poor performance occurs again, you will be suspended without pay for a period of x days."
- Summarize the meeting to avoid ambiguity or misunderstanding.
- Establish a follow-up meeting at which the associate's performance will be re-evaluated.

Termination Interviews

*F*iring people is a manager's most difficult task. You may have to terminate people after spoken and written warnings if they fail to improve their performance. Immediate termination is possible if a person

- ✓ steals
- ✓ destroys company property
- ✓ is grossly insubordinate
- ✓ falsifies time cards
- ✓ is absent for an extended period of time
- ✓ engages in criminal behaviour

Here's what you can do to make the process as painless as possible:

Before the Meeting

- Schedule the session carefully. A Monday-to-Wednesday dismissal will give the person an opportunity to set up interviews with the Unemployment Insurance office, a relocation counsellor, job search firms and her personal network.
- Avoid terminating someone on his birthday or just before Christmas. Your insensitivity will make the trauma worse.
- Determine whether the dismissal will be with or without just cause. Just cause means that you have good reason to fire the person. Without cause suggests that the reasons for termination might be more frivolous, such as a personality conflict.
- If you have just cause, decide whether you have all the necessary documentation to substantiate the dismissal, including
  - ✓ copies of written warnings
  - ✓ copies of all incidents of unacceptable performance, including dates and circumstances

- Consult legal counsel to determine the appropriate and fair severance package or notice period. The notice period will be influenced by
  - ✓ age
  - ✓ position
  - ✓ years of service
  - ✓ education
  - ✓ salary
- If the associate is being terminated for economic reasons, and is in the middle of a project, try to delay termination until the project is complete. This will not only help you, but it will give the associate a sense of achievement, which will increase her confidence when job searching.
- Prepare for the interview. Get your facts and documentation together. You may want to script what you wish to say, particularly if you have little or no experience with this process.
- Include a third party, such as a human-resources professional, to act as a witness, or provide emotional support. If you have arranged outside placement services, then you should include the counsellor.
- Conduct the meeting in a private office or room away from the eyes of fellow associates.

During the Meeting
- Limit the session to about 10 minutes.
- Show respect for the person at all times. The process is invariably devastating.
- Be brief and businesslike. Do not engage in frivolous unrelated discussion to establish rapport.
- At the outset state that the decision to terminate (with or without cause) has been made and, if appropriate, say why. Make it clear that the decision is irreversible and not open to negotiation.
- Present the facts leading up to the decision, emphasizing the nature and implication of the culminating incident.

- If the decision to terminate is economic, emphasize that the decision is not personal and that the organization will do everything reasonable to help the associate find alternative employment.
- Discuss why other alternatives were not chosen.
- Review the details of the severance package, including
  - ✓ any benefit continuance
  - ✓ the severance offer
  - ✓ release
  - ✓ reference (if appropriate)
  - ✓ any out-placement services
  - ✓ record of employment
  - ✓ final paycheque
- Do not offer a good (inaccurate) reference in return for the person's agreement to your severance package. Your misrepresentation could be a legal liability if a future employer discovers you have distorted the truth.
- Discuss why it is necessary for the person to leave immediately to avoid embarrassing meetings or justifications to colleagues.
- Allow the out-placement counsellor some time with the person to co-ordinate leaving the premises. The associate may also use this time to vent any frustration.
- Obtain any company property from the associate such as ID cards, keys, phone cards.
- Make arrangements for returning personal effects.
- Escort the person off the premises and if necessary arrange for a taxi. Alternative transportation is recommended because the person may be too upset to drive safely.

Exit Interviews

Rarely is a manager happy that an employee is leaving the company. However, you can turn a negative into a positive — conducting an exit interview with your departing colleague can provide valuable insights into ways to improve both team and process.

Before Your Associate Leaves

- Mention that you would value any opinions and insights into the working conditions at your company that could be useful to you as manager.
- Offer to set up an interview with a human resources employee if your colleague would prefer not to be interviewed by you.
- Emphasize that all information will be kept confidential.
- Schedule the interview during his last week of employment.
- Be conscious of the venue you choose, and consult your departing colleague as to where she would feel most comfortable holding the interview — long-term employees often appreciate exit luncheons outside the office. In any case, choose somewhere neutral to mitigate the "boss–subordinate" feeling.

At the Interview

- Place your associate at ease by sitting adjacent to him at a four-person table rather than directly across from him.
- Remember that you are there to listen and gather information, not to defend yourself. Take open notes. Paraphrase the occasional comment to demonstrate that you are genuinely trying to understand (see Listening).
- Encourage your colleague to be specific. Ask open-ended questions about her perceptions of your leadership style, team or

departmental interaction with management at all levels, obstacles and difficulties on the job, the culture in the company as a whole and its effect on job performance, or aspects of the job that she enjoyed. Ask if there is any other information she feels you need to know.

- Use your associate's new job as a tool to determine what circumstances could be improved. Find out about salary and benefits, the new work environment, what generally attracted him to this new position. If he is leaving without a new position lined up, this could mean either that there are compelling personal reasons or that the work environment had become intolerable. Try to elicit this information without being aggressive or patronizing.

- Thank your colleague for her time and willingness to help you make your company a better place to work. Sincerely congratulate her and wish her the best of luck.

After Your Colleague Has Left

- Organize your information in point form and pass on the most urgent problems to those who can take responsibility to fix them. Reflect on your colleague's assessment of your performance and adjust accordingly.

- If the information from the interview points to a severe or widespread problem within the department, arrange a follow-up interview with your former associate a few weeks later. His point of view may have altered once he left the organization, or his opinions may have clarified with time. Again, ask if he would prefer a human resources person as an interviewer, to get more objective information.

Exit Interview Questions

- If you had my job, what would you change first? Why?
- How could I improve our work area?
- What frustrated you most about the job?
- What did you like best about the job?
- What corporate policies do you feel are most praiseworthy?
- What corporate polices and procedures made your work life difficult? Why?
- What will your new job give you that we have not?
- What will you miss most about working here?
- If you could tell the president one thing, what would it be?
- What should we be doing to ensure that your replacement stays with us?

Unionization

If you want to make peace, you don't talk to your friends, you talk to your enemies.

MOSHE DAYAN (1915–81), LEGENDARY ISRAELI GENERAL

Organizations that do not meet the needs of their people are prone to unionization. In unionized companies people feel powerless and perceive unions as better able to help employees. But a union can reduce your flexibility with staff and interfere with your ability to communicate effectively. Here's how you can create an environment in which your people would have little interest in being unionized:

- Stay in touch with your people informally. Walk around. Ask people how things are going for them. Don't respond only to what they say, but to their body language. Probe if you feel there is a problem.
- Establish a formal process to identify and eliminate problems. For example, have a breakfast meeting with a cross section of employees each month or conduct an annual attitude survey to measure the magnitude of concerns, so that they can be tracked (see Conducting an Attitude Survey, page 179).
- Survey attitudes regularly. Break the data down by subject and control. Prioritize and deal with the items you control.
- Refer to your people in appreciative terms. "Partners" and "associates" are more endearing terms than "employees" and "subordinates."
- Continuously find new ways to improve working conditions. Encourage your associates to develop action plans for things they

have control of. Take care of other items under *your* control.

- Treat your people as equals. Share information with them about
  - ✓ finances
  - ✓ sales figures
  - ✓ new products
  - ✓ production forecasts
  - ✓ future staffing expectations
- Balance the financial goals of your business with the needs of your associates. People will not allow you to take advantage of them for a minute longer than is necessary. Share your research about salaries and benefits in your industry with your people.
- Compensate your people fairly. If business warrants it, pay them the same salaries that unionized organizations do. Your flexibility and motivated staff will give you a competitive advantage.
- Make your human resources policies known to all. If your people raise concerns about these policies, solve them quickly. If you cannot, ensure that there is a help process that is responsive, easy to access and free of retribution.
- Encourage the involvement and input of employees in human-resources program development and review. Treat employees as customers of the organization; design programs with employee interests as well as business in mind.
- Support your staff by cultivating their individual and team problem-solving skills through formal training and coaching, and recognize success in applying these skills. People who are comfortable addressing their problems themselves have less reason to look elsewhere for help in dealing with problems.

Working with Your Union

*U*nions are an important part of our labour and employment structure: they protect workers from unfair treatment and even exploitation. While their influence has been in steady decline over the past half century, it is critical for you to manage your relationship with your unionized staff effectively, to prevent costly grievances, work stoppages and strikes. Here's what you can do:

- Come to terms with the fact that your people are unionized. The chances of decertifying are remote. So learn to manage the relationship for the advantage of all concerned.
- Treat union people as part of the family, not as the enemy. Think of them as customers. People will respond positively to a constructive and open work environment.
- Treat union representatives as your peers and partners so that they will be less inclined to treat you as a foe. Your relationship must be constantly nurtured — trust takes a long time to build.
- Be prepared for ups and downs in the relationship with your union representative. However, if you consider the union a legitimate partner, the ups will be greater than the downs, and you will be able to count on its co-operation in the daily running of your area.
- Understand the differences between the union's objectives and those of your company, but look for common goals and build on them. Make sure that new initiatives can benefit all and that they do not infringe on your collective agreement. If they could, work with your union representatives to resolve the issue with win-win outcomes.

- Review your contract thoroughly. Consult your labour relations expert if you have difficulties with interpretation.
- Respect your contract: it was negotiated in good faith. Learn to live within the spirit and letter of the agreement.
- Be careful about bending rules. Bending rules establishes precedents that the union could seek to perpetuate. Do so only if there is agreement on the part of the union that this will be an exception, not the rule.
- Make sure your leadership style is based on fairness, integrity and consistency.
- If the grievances in your area are unusually high, evaluate causes and develop solutions to address concerns.
- Meet regularly with your shop steward to share information, formally or informally. Your behaviour at these encounters should indicate a sincere willingness to co-operate.
- Keep your shop steward informed of all issues affecting union workers. The more open you are, the easier it will be for you to tap into the grapevine. Often union people are better informed than managers about upcoming changes.
- If your organization wants significant changes in the next contract, work with your union representatives to prepare them and the membership for the new ideas. You can do this by
  - ✓ sharing your thinking regularly so that new ideas do not come as a surprise later on.
  - ✓ giving people articles describing how other organizations have managed similar changes successfully.
  - ✓ visiting other organizations that have made a dramatic change, to see how it has affected their people. You can then plan to avoid their mistakes.

PART VI

Performance Improvement

Mission Statements

Some organizations take weeks, months and even years to develop a mission. Using the method below, you will be able to do it in a couple of hours, over a week.

Preliminary Meeting

- Hold a meeting with your staff at which time you
  - ✓ inform them of the value of having a mission
  - ✓ explain what a mission is
  - ✓ invite them to participate in developing a mission
  - ✓ show them how it will be done and what it should contain
  - ✓ show them examples of missions
- Form a subcommittee to do the detail work, if your work area is large. If you have fewer than a dozen people, involve them all.
- Have everyone complete his or her own mission statement before your design meeting, by answering these questions:
  - ✓ Who are we? State the name of the organization, work area or team.
  - ✓ What do we do? Briefly state the nature of the product or service you provide.
  - ✓ How do we do it? Describe what you do in terms of categories such as quality, responsiveness, service, cost effectiveness or any other dimensions that you have control of.
  - ✓ For whom do we do it? Describe your customers.
  - ✓ Where do we do it? Describe the geographic territory you cover.
  - ✓ Why do we do it? Describe the benefits to the internal stakeholders, the shareholders and staff.

Decision Meeting

- Conduct a meeting to construct the mission. Get the feedback of each person and evaluate the merits of their statements. Post each on the wall. Underline useful ideas from each.
- Record the mission using the following structure:

MISSION OF

Whom _____

(Name)

What _____

(The task)

How _____

(Quality, timeliness, cost effectiveness, health and safety)

For _____

(The customer)

Where _____

(Geographic area)

Why _____

(Benefit for management and staff)

- Working line by line, take the best ideas from each statement. Write the ideas on a white board, which allows you to change and modify ideas, words and sentence structure with ease.
- Continue wordsmithing the mission until everyone is satisfied. This should not take more than an hour.

After the Meeting

- Document the mission. Circulate it to people who were not present. Ask for their feedback.
- Hold a final short meeting to add any minor finishing touches to the mission.
- Post the mission in the workplace.
- Have all staff commit to the mission by signing the statement.
- Post the mission in your meeting room to ensure that the mission has a direct bearing on all team activities.
- Identify ways of measuring the extent to which you are or are not meeting your mission. Post graphs of these indicators where everyone can see them and follow the trends.
- Celebrate your area's progress in meeting its mission. When indicators of performance decline are evident, involve your people in finding new ways to improve.

Customer Service

The purpose of organizations is to acquire and maintain customers.

THEODORE LEVITT, PROFESSOR OF BUSINESS
ADMINISTRATION EMERITUS, HARVARD BUSINESS SCHOOL

*T*he raison d'être for you and your people should be to provide superb service, quickly and in a cost-effective manner.

- Constantly make your people aware of the importance of meeting customers' needs. Customer issues should be emphasized in departmental meetings, informal discussions and on your bulletin board.
- Invite customers into your work area. Let them provide feedback on service.
- In order to remind employees about the importance of customers, place visual annotations on walls and bulletin boards. Display your mission statement, which describes
  - ✓ what you do
  - ✓ for whom
  - ✓ where (geographic area)
  - ✓ how you serve customers (quality, responsiveness, caring, value)
  - ✓ why you do what you do
- Measure critical indicators of customer satisfaction such as delivery, service and quality. Display these measures where everyone can see them. Explain the link between the mission and the measures so that people can see how they are related.

- Involve your people in the collection of data on customer service. This will help them develop ownership and responsibility for performance.
- Obtain formal feedback from your customers through written or person-to-person surveys. Analyze the data. Prioritize opportunities. Involve people in suggesting and implementing changes.
- Your best guarantee of good service is happy employees. Maintain high morale by creating a positive environment. People will respond positively if you
  - ✓ listen to them
  - ✓ keep them informed
  - ✓ acknowledge them for above average performance

In a nutshell, treat people as you would want to be treated.

- Keep your people informed about minimum customer-service standards. Your associates should know why these standards are important and should be trained to obtain them.
- When customer service improves, immediately praise your people. Conversely, when performance declines, make your team aware of the change. Seek their ideas on how to improve performance.
- Although not all customer services are easy to measure, show your appreciation when you observe your people
  - ✓ working hard to solve a problem
  - ✓ being particularly courteous
  - ✓ going the extra mile
- Make customer service a key element of your performance appraisal system. Involve your people in setting their own goals.
- Improve customer service by teaching your people skills such as
  - ✓ handling difficult customers
  - ✓ listening
  - ✓ knowing what customers want
  - ✓ problem solving
  - ✓ telephone skills

- Give your people the power to solve customer problems. As they exercise their responsibility wisely, expand their level of authority.
- Constantly ensure that your people have the power to make decisions. Give your people training and guidelines so that they can deal with problems quickly.
- Encourage your people to treat angry customers with empathy. Viewing the situation from the customer's perspective will increase enthusiasm to deal with problems without focusing on the customer's behaviour.
- Encourage and reward change. Celebrate small successes. Strive for base hits rather than home runs. Large gains will result from many small improvements, and the size of improvements will increase as your people's confidence grows.
- Always make customer service a priority. Show leadership by dropping everything when a customer problem occurs.
- Evaluate every step in your process to determine whether or not it adds value to your customer. Cut out or reduce waste. This will reduce your delivery time dramatically.
- Don't let untrained personnel deal with complex customer issues. Give them training and guidance before they mess up.
- Show you care by providing your home phone number to customers. Let them know that you do not consider it an imposition if they call for help outside business hours.
- Compare yourself with departments and organizations carrying out activities similar to your own. The more different the organization is from your own, the more you will learn. This process, known as benchmarking (see page 234), will allow you to compare measurable performance and procedures.
- Don't implement ideas from the outside without adapting them to suit your environment.

CUSTOMER FOCUS SURVEY

Answer the following questions to determine how customer-focused you are.

	Yes	No
• Have you empowered your people to deal with most customer problems without having to refer to a higher authority?	❑	❑
• Do you invite customers to your departmental meetings to give you feedback on your performance?	❑	❑
• Do you have a formal system for tracking customer complaints?	❑	❑
• Do you measure critical indicators of customer satisfaction?	❑	❑
• Do you share statistics on customer service levels with your people?	❑	❑
• Do you meet regularly with your people to continuously challenge yourself to improve levels of customer service?	❑	❑
• Do you recognize and reward outstanding customer service?	❑	❑
• Are customer service goals a part of your performance appraisal system?	❑	❑
• Do you enable and encourage your people to visit customers?	❑	❑

If you answered No to any of these questions, you have room for improvement.

Productivity

*Most people like hard work, particularly when
they're paying for it.*
FRANKLIN P. JONES (1887–1929), PRESIDENT AND CEO,
AMERICAN MANAGEMENT ASSOCIATION

Productivity — the efficiency with which we produce goods or
services — is a critical component in being competitive. Here
are some ideas to spur you to improve:

- Determine how you and your associates spend your time. Ask
  yourself what percentage of the time was spent carrying out activities directly related to your objectives. Anything less than 95%
  suggests a problem.
- Have clear goals (see Group Goal Setting, page 244). Share these
  with your people. Encourage them to spend time achieving these
  goals. Break the goals down into individual goals.
- Measure progress towards goals. Record these and post them so
  that people can see changes.
- Encourage associates to measure their own productivity so that
  they will feel responsibility for their own performance.
- Listen to and implement new ideas that enable you and your
  people to work smarter, not harder. Allow people to try new
  ideas.
- Give recognition for suggestions. Share new ideas with others in
  your team so that they can benefit, too.
- Evaluate key processes regularly. Involve your people in documenting all steps on a process map (see Process Improvement,
  page 238). Evaluate the map by asking

✓ Is each step necessary?

✓ Is there duplication?

✓ Does each step add value?

✓ Where do we experience most delays?

- Focus on doing jobs right the first time. Doing things quickly will lead to mistakes, which result in poor customer service and lower productivity.

- Find the best way to do a job. Document it. Then train your people to do the job right. Encourage people to follow the most efficient procedure.

- Cross-train people so that they can help one another when work piles up at one work station. Flexible workers can also fill in for others during breaks, vacations and sick leave.

- Don't automate for the sake of automation. Make the process as simple and efficient as possible before you consider replacing manual tasks with machines.

- Cut out unnecessary meetings. Hold informal meetings in the office or on the shop floor that last no more than five to ten minutes.

- Evaluate the necessity for the paperwork you do. Ask yourself

  ✓ Does anybody read it?

  ✓ Does anyone care about the information?

  ✓ Do the data prompt decision making?

  If the answer to any of these questions is No, fight to simplify or eliminate the report.

- Organize the work area. Put things where they are clearly visible or can be found easily. Searching for documents often takes up to 30% of people's time.

- Review the sequence of activities in your work area. Move people so that the process flows better. Also, move people who work together closer to one another to improve communications and reduce material handling.

- Don't hire more people at peak periods. Get temporary staff. Better still, review procedures to see if you can simplify them and reduce work.

- Benchmark your processes (see Benchmarking, page 234). Benchmarking will enable you to compare
  - ✓ measurable indicators of performance
  - ✓ methods and procedures
- You can compare the things you do with
  - ✓ similar work areas in your organization
  - ✓ similar work areas in other organizations
  - ✓ different work areas in other organizations
- The more willing you are to compare yourself with different organizations and the more receptive you are to radically new ideas, the more opportunities you will have. For example, comparing line-up times at a hydro payment receipts office with those at a hotel check-in desk will reveal more opportunities than comparing them with line-up times at another hydro office.
- Modify new ideas so that they fit your own circumstances.

QUESTIONS THAT POINT TO IMPROVEMENT

Review the following questions with your associates to uncover ideas for improving productivity.

- Is each step in our process necessary?
- Does each step add value for our customers?
- Are some activities missing?
- Do people check their own work or is it left to someone else at completion?
- Is the work flow logical?
- Are related activities positioned next to each other?
- Do we have policies and procedures that prevent improvements?
- Do people have the power to make improvements in their own jobs?
- Do we measure productivity?
- Do we share productivity data with our operators?
- Have we involved our people in finding ideas to improve productivity?
- Do we have unnecessary levels of approval?
- Where does the process stop for the longest time? Why?
- Where are the bottlenecks? How can they be removed?

Project Management

Crisis is another name for opportunity.

ANONYMOUS

*P*rojects attract disaster the way the Royal Family attracts bad biographers. With a little luck and care, however, you can keep your project from landing in your company's garbage bin.

Develop a specific and detailed mandate.

- Determine the aim of the project (to research, recommend or implement change, for example).
- Establish the parameters of the project: geographic, departmental, authoritative.
- List the areas affected by the project: which organizational levels, which products or services, which systems and processes.
- Assemble the best team. Ask yourself these questions:
  - ✓ Are the team members representative of the departments affected by the project?
  - ✓ Do they have enough time available to participate fully in the project?
  - ✓ Is there a good distribution of relevant and helpful skill sets?
  - ✓ Do the people involved have a good grasp of the fields covered by the project? As an obvious example, if part of the project is setting up a database, you will need, at the least, an expert in information architecture and one in the specific field from which the data will be drawn.
  - ✓ Is a variety of viewpoints and methodologies represented?
  - ✓ Do the team and the project have a sponsor?

Meet with your team.

- Welcome your team and explain the project mandate, its importance, the parameters, the composition of its team and your overall plan. Get buy-in.
- Create ground rules that establish how the team will work together. (For example, "We will be open to new ideas, allow everybody to participate fully, and notify the project leader in advance if we have fallen behind schedule in reaching a goal.")
- Draw up some organizational guidelines: when you will meet, how often and where. These should grow naturally from the plan's goal breakdown. It is essential to get team buy-in to these structures.
- Quickly brainstorm to anticipate potential obstacles and roadblocks and incorporate ways to overcome them in the overall plan.
- End the meeting on a positive note by enumerating the benefits to team members of the success of the project.

Develop a plan.

- Working with the team, break the project down into measurable, quantifiable steps (goals), and make each step essential to the completion of the project.
- Use appropriate tracking tools to document your plan. There are many sophisticated yet simple software packages that will enable to you produce Gant charts or PERT (Program Evaluation and Review Technique) charts to guide and monitor your activities. (Gant charts describe in detail the different tasks, who's going to do them and the beginning and completion dates. PERT charts describe all the steps that need to be taken to complete a task, as well as the critical path, which, if delayed, will delay the entire project.)
- Set specific deadlines for each step. (ASAP doesn't qualify as a deadline.)
- Assign specific people to each goal.

- Determine the basic roadmap for reaching each goal.
- Get endorsement of the plan from the project sponsor.

Manage the process.

- Monitor progress through the achievement of the plan's subsidiary goals. Make a visual progress chart to encourage team members and boost morale.
- Supervise, don't substitute. If someone is not doing the work, replace him or her or call in additional resources and personnel. Your task is to manage your team, be a role model (stay out of office and departmental politics), focus on the big picture and link it to an overall vision and run inclusive and concise meetings that follow specific agendas.
- Issue periodic progress reports to team members to boost morale and make them feel appreciated.
- Recognize individual excellence, and transmit this commendation to the team and the person's boss.
- Modify the project plan and parameters as necessary.

Project Management 911

You can give a problematic project a final push towards completion by

- ✓ increasing your effort input to output ratio by a factor of 10 (doing 10 times the work you think is necessary)
- ✓ bringing in the cavalry — a friend, mentor or colleague who can support and advise you)
- ✓ maintaining forward momentum — by moving forward every week, you will drag the rest of the project with you
- ✓ including focus groups of primary consumers and modifying project aims and parameters to create extraordinary outcomes based on their information
- ✓ keeping a reserve — try to allow about twice as much for time and expenses as you really need

Wrap up.

- Present your project findings to senior management to get buy-in and recognition.
- Celebrate the conclusion in an appropriate way. A meal or gift vouchers are two ways to thank your team members.

Benchmarking

*The best measure of one's talents is often how
your peers grade your work.*

<small>AUTOMOTIVE INDUSTRIES MAGAZINE</small>

*E*very business, no matter what its size, requires continual self-
assessment and self-improvement to stay ahead of the game or,
quite frequently, to stay in the game at all. This process of evaluation is known as benchmarking. It consists of five steps performed in
an ongoing cycle designed to measure which processes deliver, and
which need to be improved.

Identify.

* Benchmarking measures success or failure in specific areas of a
  business; it is your first task to identify these productive (or problem, as the case may be) areas. Some possible candidates for
  benchmarking are
  * ✓ customer complaint levels
  * ✓ product or service quality
  * ✓ sales and market share and
  * ✓ fixed (plant) and variable (labour) costs
* Remember that the areas must be amenable to quantitative as
  well as qualitative measurement — otherwise, you are wasting
  your time and that of others. Certain areas of measurement will
  require specific types of information.
* Your second task is to identify, based on the measured areas, what
  kind of information you will need to amass. Some examples are
  * ✓ level of quality control
  * ✓ efficiency in production and distribution

- ✓ workplace safety
- ✓ employee morale

Plan.

- How do you go about collecting the data you need? Do you need an ad hoc benchmarking committee, or a permanent team? Who should be involved, and at what point of the process? These are the first questions you must answer to develop your assessment plan.
- The benchmarking team (permanent or otherwise) should include at least three people, and some or all of the following:
  - ✓ senior managers who will be responsible for authorizing any changes
  - ✓ front-line employee representatives to contribute to both data collection and process changes based on the results
  - ✓ an outside facilitator to ensure objectivity and that the process is followed quickly and effectively
- Data can be collected in a number of ways — using more than one of these ways will enhance the value of the information you receive:
  - ✓ surveys
  - ✓ checklists detailing key activities you are monitoring
  - ✓ impartial observation of workplace behaviour (this will require calling in a professional consultant)
  - ✓ telephone and/or e-mail interviews
- Information can also be collected from a variety of sources, some so obvious that they are often overlooked:
  - ✓ your own organization (internal and external employees, company newsletters, etc.)
  - ✓ current competitors' employees, and your own employees who have recently worked for competitors
  - ✓ industry and trade conferences, journals and other publications
  - ✓ business books and articles published for the trade

Implement.

- Before beginning the data collection, have a team or division meeting and present your plan. Take suggestions and comments as needed. Don't forget to contact sources of information outside your organization to encourage them to participate. Offer them access to the collected data if necessary.
- Put your plan into action efficiently and with a minimum of disruption to routine. If the method of data collection is long-term (for example, weekly departmental checklists), encourage employees to incorporate it into their routine, and institute regular meetings of the benchmarking team to collate and evaluate the data.
- Start planning for change right away, even before the results come in. (It is axiomatic that if you set out to discover problems and inefficiencies, you will find them.)
- Have the team post regular updates on the benchmarking process on company e-mail or on the general bulletin boards to keep employees interested and apprised.
- Plan the first "information session" for a week after the final (or first) batch of results are due to come in, and make the date known to all.

Evaluate.

- Have the team collect all the available data and assemble it into tables or graphs. This will allow you to focus quickly on areas of concern and go right to proposing potential solutions.
- Make sure that the breakdown of the data is specific as well as general — there is no use determining that the warehouse chronically ships product late if you don't know what product, to whom, when or why. As well, prepare the data so that industry standards are clearly delineated — this is a quick way to determine how far you have to go to improve poor performance.
- Once you have the data tabulated, do two things: post the results for the employees to see, and start brainstorming solutions to

whatever shortfalls you have discovered. That way, when you have your first "information session," you will be armed with solutions but flexible enough to incorporate suggestions from those at the meeting.

- After the first "information session," regroup your team, hammer out the final plans for change and present them at a staff meeting.
- Make sure that responsibility for implementing these changes is clearly assigned at the meeting.
- Specify a certain period of time after which you expect the shortfall to be turned around based on the solutions you have presented. This could be as long as one or two years, or as short as a month.
- Don't stop collecting data. Make it an ongoing process. You will need information to continue the benchmarking and improvement cycle.

Identify (measure success/failure).

- Continue collecting data on the areas you have identified up until the deadline for the turnaround. Then, look again at the most recent data and determine the success or failure of your plans. Based on this evaluation (it should probably be done in conjunction with the team, and incorporated into a staff meeting), identify new areas needing improvement or new solutions to persistent problem areas.
- If necessary, alter the membership of the benchmark team to reflect changes in focus. Now repeat the cycle.

Process Improvement

When a business can pioneer a production process that is effective at reducing cost, enhancing quality, or both, a sustainable competitive advantage can be created.

DAVID A. AAKER, AUTHOR OF
DEVELOPING BUSINESS STRATEGIES

Studies of processes find that activities that add value for customers take place only 5% of the time. So the opportunity to reduce cycle and delivery time is enormous. Here is how you can work with your people to improve process radically:

Step 1: Identify an opportunity.
- Find a process that can be improved. This will not be difficult — they all can be improved! More likely you will need to prioritize your opportunities. As a guide, pick a process that
  - ✓ is causing customer frustration and complaints
  - ✓ could save significant dollars if improved
  - ✓ relates to the department and the corporate mission
  - ✓ is relatively simple to solve

Step 2: Form a team.
- Invite six to ten people to help you improve the process. The team should represent all stages of the process and contain people from two or more departments. Select people who
  - ✓ understand the process
  - ✓ are concerned about improvement

- ✓ represent each stage of the process
- ✓ will make the time to work on the team
- ✓ have the power to make changes
- If your team consists of front-line people, you will need a mandate from a senior manager to make changes. Such a mandate will give participants the feeling that their hard work will not be in vain.
- Hold your first team meeting. At the kickoff you should
  - ✓ introduce members to one another
  - ✓ explain the process and the steps you will be taking
  - ✓ train people in the tools of process mapping
  - ✓ get commitments from each person regarding their participation

Step 3: Map the process.

- Give people a week to collect information about the process from the perspective of their work area.
- At your next meeting, record all the steps of the process on a white board. The board should be pre-drawn, with the people who are involved listed on the left and the time on the bottom.
- Note the opinions of participants as you guide them through the steps of the process. Record activities, starting on the left side and moving to the right. Write each activity or decision on a Post-it Note. The advantage of Post-its is that they can be moved easily. If you are unsure about any part of the map, leave it blank and continue. You can do detailed research later.
- Use appropriate symbols for each step in the process. The most commonly used icons are:

ACTIVITY   DECISION   DOCUMENT   DELAY

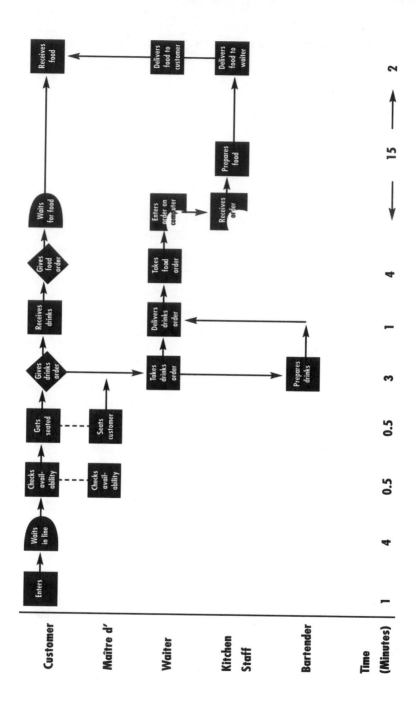

- The process map should show
  - ✓ each step
  - ✓ the inputs and outputs of each step
  - ✓ all decisions
  - ✓ the people involved
  - ✓ the time to do each step
- Make a draft of the process and allow team members an opportunity to confirm its accuracy with their peers.

Step 4: Analyze the process.

- At your next meeting, adjust the process based on feedback from team members.
- Benchmark your process to determine just how ineffective it is (see Benchmarking, page 234). If it is completely ineffective, consider scrapping it. If it requires fine-tuning, analyze it step-by-step.
- Analyze the process by determining whether
  - ✓ each step is necessary
  - ✓ the flow is logical
  - ✓ each step adds value
  - ✓ some activities are missing
  - ✓ some steps are wasteful
  - ✓ there is duplication
- List the problems. Prioritize them based on their impact on the customer, their cost and their time requirements.
- Taking one problem at a time, find the major cause(s). These typically are people, methods, materials or machinery (equipment).
- Solve the major cause(s).

Step 5: Redesign the process.

- Based on the team's ideas, redraw the process map to reduce waste, duplication and time.

Step 6: Implement change.

- Develop action plans for all the improvements.
- Spread the changes among as many people as possible to ensure that the workload is evenly distributed.
- Hold meetings with all those affected to make sure that they
  - ✓ understand the changes
  - ✓ agree to the changes
  - ✓ will make the changes

Step 7: Monitor and hold gains.

- Follow up with people to make sure that changes are being implemented.
- Encourage and recognize effort to reduce the difficulties usually associated with change.

Step 8: Measure the results.

- Keep a tally of the improvements. Charting them and displaying them for everyone to see will promote pride in all those responsible. It will also increase enthusiasm for your next process-improvement project.

PROCESS IMPROVEMENT ROADMAP

STEP 1
Identify an opportunity.

STEP 2
Form a team.

STEP 3
Map the process.

STEP 4
Analyze the process.

STEP 5
Redesign the process.

STEP 6
Implement change.

STEP 7
Monitor and hold gains.

STEP 8
Measure the results.

Group Goal Setting

> *You've got to be very careful if you don't know where you are going, because you may not get there.*
>
> YOGI BERRA, AMERICAN BASEBALL LEGEND

*W*ithout goals, managers and the people around them are doomed to operate aimlessly, adding little value to the organization. Sometimes we set goals unrealistically high and at other times our goals are too modest. These guidelines will help you set goals correctly:

- Review the mission of your organization. Identify the key elements that can be measured. For example, if your mission stated, "We are committed to exceeding our customers' needs by providing high quality products on time. This goal will enable us to satisfy our shareholders and provide an environment of security and growth for our staff," you would identify indicators of
  - ✓ quality
  - ✓ delivery
  - ✓ shareholders' return
  - ✓ staff security and growth
- Call an employee meeting. Explain the importance of setting goals.
- Ask for input regarding critical indicators of performance. As a guide, choose four to six indicators covering critical areas of the mission.
- Establish current performance levels by taking the average of the previous few months.

- Set goals. These will be most valuable if they are SMART:
  - ✓ Specific
  - ✓ Measurable
  - ✓ Agreed-upon
  - ✓ Realistic
  - ✓ Time-based
- Set mini-goals if goals are large. Smaller goals allow you to celebrate successes more often. Each stepping stone should bring you closer to your final goal.
- Use benchmarking. Compare your goals with those set by other departments or organizations doing similar work.
- Develop action plans that will lead to improved performance. Ask for your people's input. List all the actions together with dates by which they must be completed. Get volunteers to undertake the tasks.
- If your staff doesn't volunteer to help, you can do one of a number of things to involve them:
  - ✓ Find out why there is a reluctance to get involved. Remove any obstacles that your people identify
  - ✓ Delegate jobs to specific people. Saying "Mark, would you do ____?" will get a better response than "Who would like to do ____?"
  - ✓ Get agreement from your associates to spread the workload. Have them undertake tasks on a rotation basis.
- Display goals in a clearly visible place to maintain awareness and focus.
- Review performance regularly. Compare it with goals.
- If performance is improving, praise those responsible.
- If performance is not improving, find out why. Involve your people in adjusting goals to a more realistic level or, better still, find new ways of achieving your existing goals.

Strategic Planning

> *Business, more than any other occupation, is a continual dealing with the future: it is a continual calculation, an instinctive exercise in foresight.*
>
> HENRY R. LUCE (1898–1967),
> AMERICAN EDITOR AND PUBLISHER

Strategic planning is an activity usually considered the domain of senior managers. But all managers need to think and act strategically so that they can influence the future rather than be impacted by it. The steps you must take to develop a plan are set out below. Customize them to suit your work environment.

Step 1: Plan to plan.

Strategic planning is a slow, difficult process. Before you begin, ask yourself

- ✓ how much time you can devote to the process, including research and documentation
- ✓ what support you will need from those above and below and from your peers
- ✓ to what extent you are able to involve the people who must help you implement changes
- ✓ to what extent you want to involve those who can implement change
- ✓ what steps you will take
- ✓ when you want to complete the plan
- ✓ what you will do with the plan when it is complete

Step 2: Develop a vision and a mission.

- Create a vision statement. The vision represents what you *aspire* to become. This will typically be a short one-line statement that represents the dream of the leadership team. The statement may not be entirely possible or practical, but it will galvanize the energy and focus of the staff. Words such as "World Leader," "The Benchmark," "World Class," and "Most Respected" are appropriate in the vision.
- Create a mission statement (see Mission Statements, page 219). Work with your team to develop a statement of what you do daily. The statement should be a pragmatic description of how you will satisfy all stakeholders (customers, management and staff). Your mission should be
  - ✓ easily understood
  - ✓ short — not longer than two or three sentences
  - ✓ fairly specific, so that it will prompt goal setting and tracking
  - ✓ general enough that it will not date
- Ensure that everyone agrees on the content.
- Post the mission statement in a prominent place and have all staff members sign their names to it. This will symbolize their agreement.

Step 3: Evaluate your present position.

- Look at your operating statistics to evaluate your costs, quality, responsiveness, morale, and health and safety.
- Compare yourself to others around you to develop a sense of how bad or good you are.
- Conduct interviews one on one or in groups to find out
  - ✓ what frustrates people when they deal with you
  - ✓ what infuriates them
  - ✓ how user-friendly customer services are
  - ✓ what policies prevent people from doing their best

Step 4: Build a model for success.

- Based on your research in Step 3, create a model for success. The critical elements may be as shown in the diagram below.
- Working with your people, identify indicators to track your progress (see Measuring Team Performance, page 91). Encourage your people to pick indicators in the categories of
  - ✓ quality/service
  - ✓ timeliness/responsiveness
  - ✓ costs/value
  - ✓ health and safety
  - ✓ morale

  You should not have more than two indicators in each category otherwise you'll spend too much time on data collection, leaving you little time for analyzing, planning and taking corrective action.
- Ensure that your chosen indicators relate specifically to your intentions as outlined in your mission.

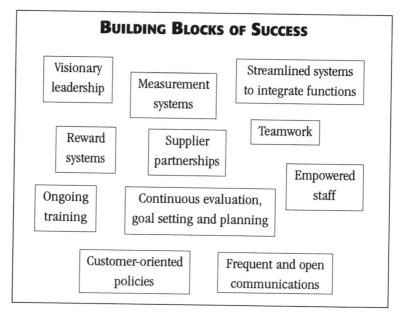

BUILDING BLOCKS OF SUCCESS

Visionary leadership	Measurement systems	Streamlined systems to integrate functions
Reward systems	Supplier partnerships	Teamwork
Ongoing training	Continuous evaluation, goal setting and planning	Empowered staff
	Customer-oriented policies	Frequent and open communications

- The best indicators in each category will be those that are
  - ✓ easy to collect
  - ✓ accurate
  - ✓ already being collected
  - ✓ measurable
  - ✓ something the team can influence
- If you have picked an indicator that is not being measured, set up a data collection system and get your people to take responsibility for collection.

Step 5: Set goals.

- Set goals together with your associates. Your goals should be SMART:
  - ✓ **S**pecific
  - ✓ **M**easurable
  - ✓ **A**greed-upon
  - ✓ **R**ealistic
  - ✓ **T**ime-specific
- Post the goals and your current level of performance for everyone to see.

Step 6: Develop plans for improvement.

- Develop specific plans to achieve goals with your people.
- For plans to be achieved in the next 12 months, list all actions, who will do them, and the dates by which they will be done. Also list people who will be affected by those decisions so that they will be informed.
- Post plans in your work area so that everyone is aware of them. Delete each item as it is dealt with.
- Identify milestones for longer range goals. For example, you might want to establish preventive maintenance programs for 60% of your equipment by year 2, 90% by year 3, and 100% by year 4.

Step 7: Identify threats and plan to remove them.

- Create a list of obstacles that will prevent you from meeting your goals. Prioritize them. Categorize those that you have control over and those you don't.
- Focus on key roadblocks that you *do* control. Develop specific actions to deal with them.
- Work with those outside your work area whose goodwill you will need to remove roadblocks you don't control.

Ongoing Scanning of the Environment.

- While you are going through Steps 1 to 7, look outside your work area for trends and changes that will affect you or which you could take advantage of.
- Encourage your people to help identify real or potential changes in the environment by
  - ✓ circulating articles of interest
  - ✓ subscribing to and circulating trade journals
  - ✓ attending conferences
  - ✓ visiting trade shows
  - ✓ visiting competitors
  - ✓ visiting customers

Strategic Planning Roadmap

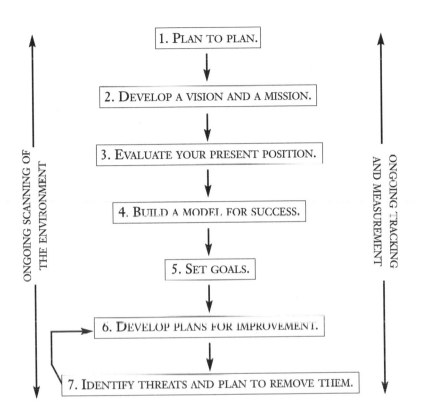

1. Plan to plan.

2. Develop a vision and a mission.

3. Evaluate your present position.

4. Build a model for success.

5. Set goals.

6. Develop plans for improvement.

7. Identify threats and plan to remove them.

ONGOING SCANNING OF THE ENVIRONMENT

ONGOING TRACKING AND MEASUREMENT

THE 10 GOLDEN RULES OF STRATEGIC PLANNING

1. Involve everyone you need to carry out your plan.
2. Document your plan.
3. Keep the process alive by updating it continuously. Modify your plan as needed.
4. Keep your plan visual by posting your mission, indicators and action plans.
5. Work collaboratively with those outside your work area whose help you will need.
6. Remember why you are developing your plan: it is to help you acquire and improve service to your customers.
7. Make sure your plan fits in with senior management's goals.
8. Keep it simple.
9. Don't undertake too much. Taking on too much leads to nonperformance, disillusionment, skepticism and failure.
10. Spread your action plans so that they will be done in an orderly manner.

Outsourcing

Outsourcing presents a quick and effective way to farm out non-core activities on the road to becoming a virtual organization.

ANONYMOUS

*M*anagers are constantly looking for new ways to serve customers better, faster and at less cost. Sometimes the task seems daunting, particularly after the failure of new initiatives. Under such circumstances, it may be appropriate to look outside the organization for solutions, by partnering with an outside supplier.

Around the world, outsourcing is becoming increasingly easier with the daily improvement of Internet technology, which now allows people to communicate visually and verbally on demand. It is now possible to build a "virtual" organization, with organizations around the world collaborating on common work processes.

Outsourcing is a senior management decision, and one that is strategic in nature. As a senior manager, consider these advantages of outsourcing:

- Organizations that specialize in one area, such as training or information services or transportation, generally come closer to perfecting their systems, and have lower costs as a consequence. Their tendency towards continuous innovation ensures world-class capability.

- Outsourcing gives you access to know-how. Your organization cannot excel in everything it does. Focus on those areas that really impact on your success, while leaving some of the other "non-core" aspects to specialists.

- Placing operations that are not key to your organization's future under the umbrella of a capable management team will allow you to focus on the things you do best.
- Outsourcing conserves resources by allowing you to redirect your own people, capital and time to activities that provide customers with the most value.
- External organizations can provide essential resources for companies that do not have the time or money to invest in state-of-the-art equipment or in developing expertise.
- Outsourcing accelerates the re-engineering process. Redesigning and streamlining work processes is a lot easier on paper than it is to implement. Getting buy-in from all stakeholders to changes is difficult. Getting them to implement and maintain those changes is even more difficult.
- Outsourcing helps you gain control of functions that are poorly managed. Some functions are so complex that they are vulnerable to crisis if a few key people leave. Placing these operations outside your organization alleviates this problem.
- Organizations entering into a partnership share any risk that may be involved, such as a loss of key people or changes in technology.
- Outsourcing can make capital funds available. Your operations, technology and equipment may have value to an outside vendor. This could bring about a cash infusion that can be applied to more profitable areas of operations.

The timing of outsourcing is important. Consider delaying outsourcing if
- There is a danger of losing know-how. Outsourcing a strategically important function may be costly if the relationship falters and you need to bring the function back into your organization.
- You're not ready to let go. Evaluate your need for control. If you are uncomfortable with letting go, outsourcing may cause you sleepless nights — and a bad relationship with the outside vendor.

- The real cost exceeds your own. The cost of outsourcing is not simply the invoices submitted by an outside vendor. To these add the cost of the time and resources expended on managing the relationship.
- You're looking for a quick fix. It is unlikely that you will experience an overnight reversal of performance with someone else in the driver's seat. Band-Aid solutions might appear to stop the bleeding, but the problem will continue to fester beneath the surface.
- You need flexibility. Outsourcing companies tend to specialize and excel at a few things. They cannot be all things to all people.

If you are a middle or first-level manager, your strategy must be to avoid outsourcing of your own and your team's jobs. Here's how you can help your cause:
- Benchmark your performance against the best practices of people inside and outside your industry. This exercise will not only give you a sense of how effective you are, but will also tell you whether your costs are in line with those to be had outside your organization.
- Improve the performance of your work area to match the best available.
- Involve your staff in finding new and improved ways to serve your customers.
- Measure your performance. Develop and monitor your effectiveness using indicators that track
  - ✓ the quality of your product
  - ✓ the quality of your service to internal and external customers
  - ✓ the timeliness of your service
  - ✓ how cost-effective you are
  - ✓ the level of morale in your area
  - ✓ how safe and healthy your operations are
- Keep key decision makers aware of the progress you are making.

Index

About the Author

Cy Charney is an internationally respected consultant, adult educator, and author. President of Charney and Associates Inc., he has developed a variety of unique interventions to help organizations in both the private and public sector to become leaders in their field. His clients include a number of Fortune 500 companies and government departments around the world.

Charney is a frequent keynote speaker at conferences. He is also a seasoned trainer, who customizes a variety of programs, always with the intention of adding value for internal and external customers. His training interventions include a learning system called Peer Monitoring™, a method of self-directed learning for groups in which team members train each other without a professional facilitator. One of the tools used in this learning system is *The Instant Manager.*

Cy is a member of the faculty of the executive programs of the Schulich School of Business at York University, the University of British Columbia, Saint Mary's University, the University of Alberta, and the University of Northern British Columbia, and conducts workshops for the Canadian Management Centre in Toronto.

Charney has published some two dozen articles and is the author of six books, including *The Manager's Tool Kit, The Portable Mentor, The Instant Sales Pro*, and is co-author of *The Trainer's Tool Kit.*

Mr. Charney has an undergraduate arts degree in psychology, a Masters in business leadership, and a Public Administrator designation from The Institute of Chartered Secretaries and Administrators in Canada. He lives in Thornhill, near Toronto. For more information, contact Charney at www.askcharney.com.